MW01620837

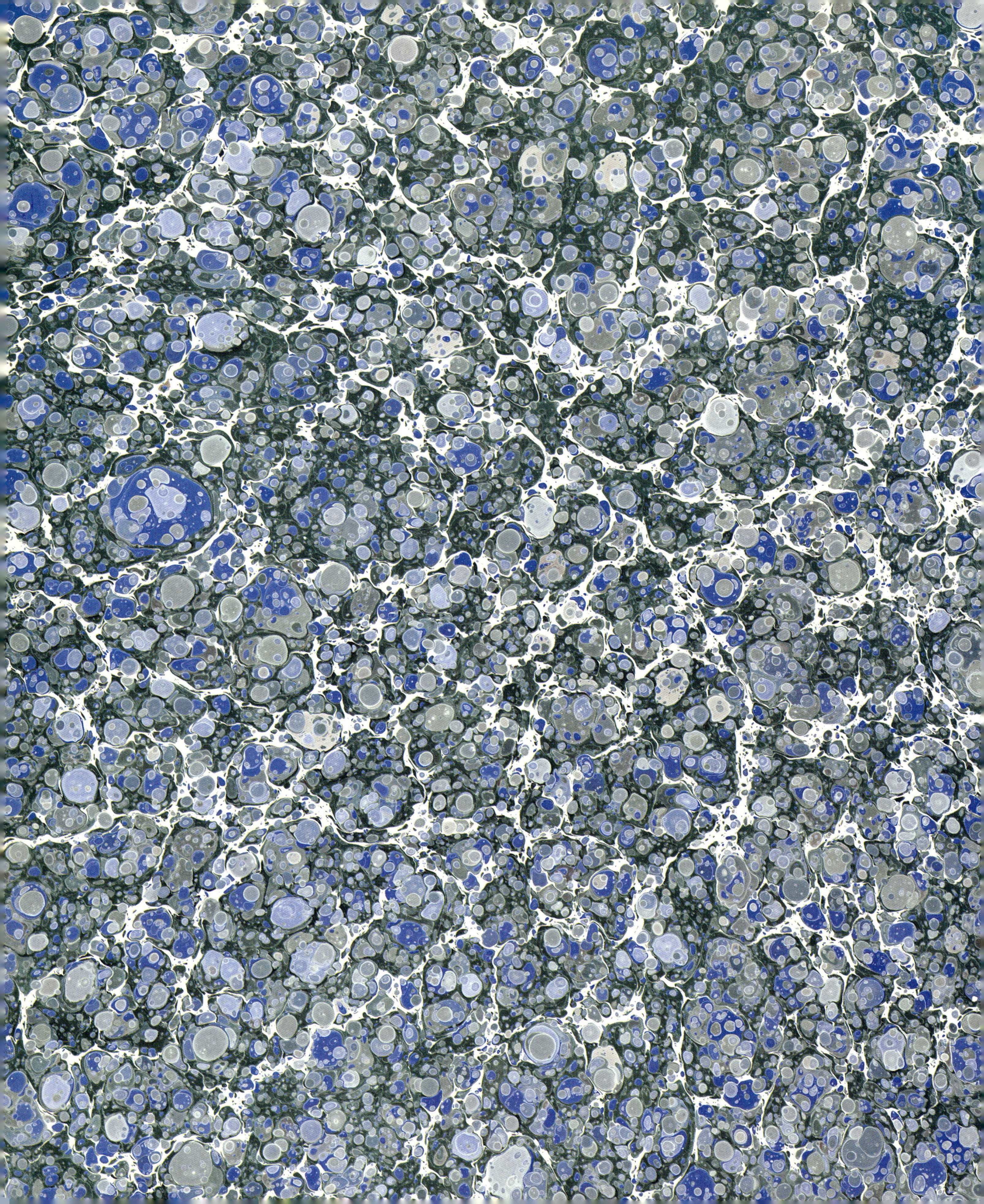

The Ultimate
MARBLING
HANDBOOK
A Guide to Basic and Advanced Techniques
for Marbling Paper and Fabric
DIANE MAURER-MATHISON
WATSON-GUPTILL PUBLICATIONS
New York

Notes on the Art

On cover: "Escher's Octopus" by the author. Classical watercolor marbling done on a carrageenan size.

On endpapers: A watercolor-marbled Scallop pattern done on a carrageenan size, by the author.

On pages 2–3: A watercolor-marbled Stone pattern done on a carrageenan size, by the author.

All line art provided by Paul Maurer and Jeffery Mathison.

Acknowledgments

Thanks to all the marbling artists who shared their secrets, their expertise, and photographs of their inspiring works. Special thanks to Laura Crandall, Jeffery Mathison, Paul Maurer, Marie Palowoda, Kay Radcliffe, and Ingrid Weimann.

Senior Editor: Candace Raney
Editor: Julie Mazur
Designer: Jay Anning
Production Manager: Ellen Greene

First published in 1999 by Watson-Guptill Publications,
a division of BPI Communications, Inc.,
1515 Broadway, New York, N.Y. 10036

Library of Congress Cataloging-in-Publication Data

Maurer-Mathison, Diane V., 1944–
The ultimate marbling handbook: a guide to basic and advanced techniques for marbling paper and fabric / by Diane Maurer-Mathison.
p. cm.
Includes bibliographical references and index.
ISBN 0-8230-5575-2
1. Textile painting. 2. Marbling. 3. Marbled papers. I. Title.
TT851.M38 1999
745.7—dc21 98-47000
CIP

Manufactured in Singapore

First printing, 1999

1 2 3 4 5 6 7 8 9 / 07 06 05 04 03 02 01 00 99

For Jennifer

"The Star," by Kay Radcliffe, 6 x 7 inches (15.2 x 17.8 cm).
Drawing over oil marbling on a carrageenan size.

Contents

PREFACE

The art of marbling has grown at an amazing pace since it first captured my interest in the early 1980s. At that time there were only a few sketchy magazine articles on the craft and some mention of the marbling process in antique books, hidden away in rare book rooms of university libraries. In 1984, when my marbling partner Paul Maurer and I self-published our booklet *An Introduction to Carrageenan & Watercolor Marbling*, only a handful of craftspeople were marbling, usually to produce cover papers for their bookbinding projects.

Most people in those early marbling days had never heard of the craft. They would look at you with a blank stare if you identified yourself as a "marbler." I carried a small folio of papers to show people what marbling looked like and impressed quite a few, who at first thought I created the complicated designs by painting them with a tiny brush. When I explained that the colors were floated on a liquid and patterned with combs and rakes, people were only slightly less impressed and wanted to know where they could learn to make such beautiful designs.

Paul and I began teaching and, after gaining some expertise, many of our students held their own classes. Because an interest in crafts and handmade papers was growing, a handful of other veteran marblers across the country also began holding workshops. Interest in marbling grew exponentially as students became teachers, spawning a second generation of students and teachers. *Ink & Gall*, a quarterly marbling journal (no longer published) appeared, and professional marblers began holding yearly conventions that drew hundreds of marblers from around the world.

When manufacturers and advertising agencies saw the new designs, marbled patterns began appearing everywhere. Galleries and museum shops showed marbled jewelry, books, and scarves, and manufacturers placed marbling on everything from greeting cards to tissue boxes. Unfortunately, in the rush to market designs and show the latest trends in fashion and furnishings, some technically deficient work was put before the public, highlighting dust spots, shift marks, and grainy patterns.

Would-be marblers learned that although marbling was easier than painting in each little loop and turn in a design, it was by no means an instant art that guaranteed professional results. Although certain types of marbling, like suminagashi or oil color marbling, could be tamed more quickly, it could take months or even years of practice to produce fine classical watercolor-marbled designs. Even then, as every marbler eventually learns, you might be visited by an ornery marbling muse (usually beckoned by a change in atmospheric conditions) who can suddenly make your colors run, spread, or behave in a way you've never seen before.

A watercolor-marbled Reverse Bouquet design done on a carrageenan size, by the author

Detail of "Crash Marbleized Paper" by German marbler Gabriele Grünebaum, 17 x 23¼ inches (43 x 59 cm). Gabriele floated oil color paints on a hot size to create this striking image.

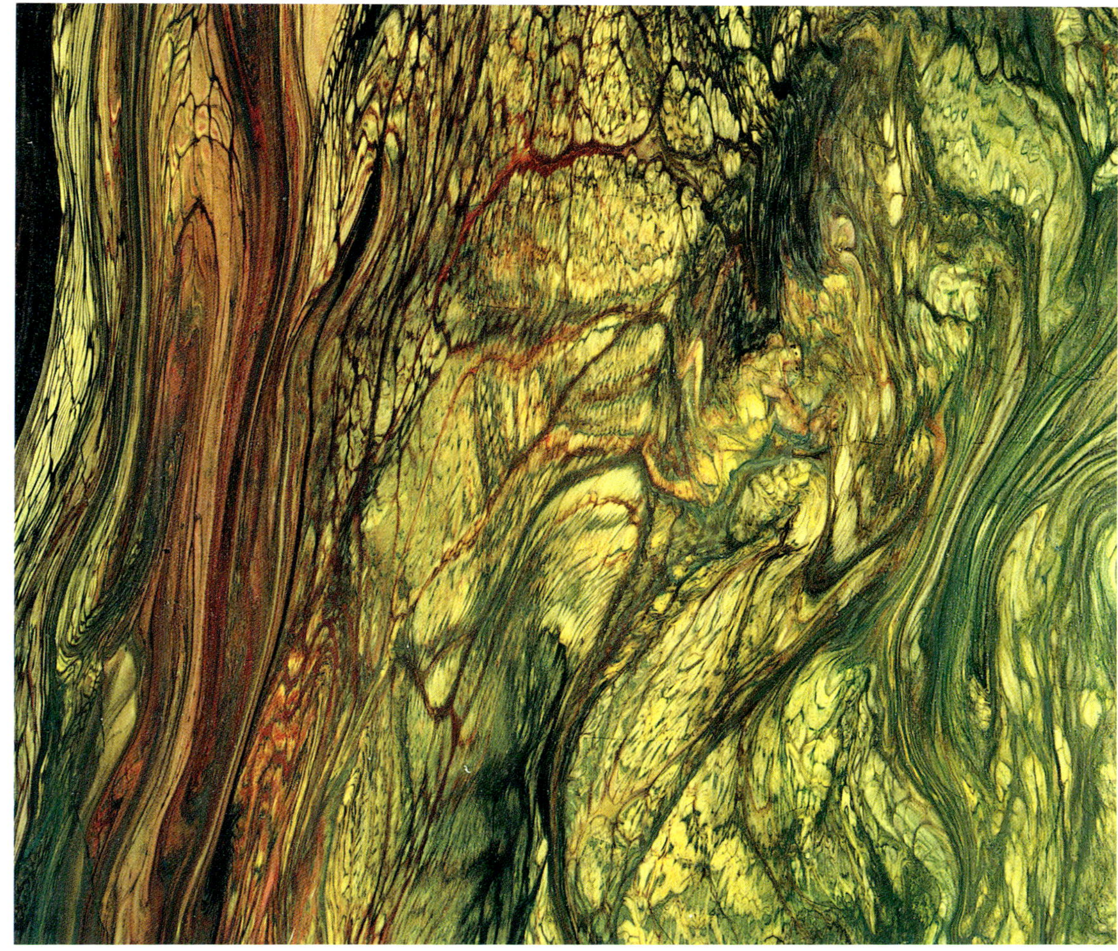

In my second marbling book, *Marbling: A Complete Guide to Creating Beautiful Patterned Papers and Fabrics* (published in 1991), I mentioned the marbling muse and the frustration marblers can feel if they don't "go with the flow" at these times, following the muse into experimental work and saving the project at hand for another day. Many readers wrote to tell me that they did some of their most satisfying and creative marbling on "off days," when they relinquished control and let the medium guide them into the uncharted territory of "extreme" marbling.

Although most of my workshop students are thrilled with the magic of marbling and the process of creating classical marbled designs, many are also eager to break the rules and try some more artful, unconventional designs. Painters and collage artists seem particularly interested in creating unusual images that they can incorporate into their art, and many have written to ask if I have a book that focuses on more avant-garde image-making. *The Ultimate Marbling Handbook* is designed to fill this need, while still providing solid instruction in classical marbling.

The Ultimate Marbling Handbook can guide novice marblers though an exciting exploration of all types of marbling. With practice, you can use this book to become technically proficient and to produce stunning papers and fabrics. If you're already marbling and are having difficulty fine-tuning your work, the extensive troubleshooting guide in each section can help you approach and solve specific problems. And, if you're among the first generation of marblers who've already learned the basics and are becoming just a tad bored with the medium, this handbook can help revive your interest with new tricks and techniques from marblers around the world.

Introduction

The roots of marbling extend at least as far back as twelfth-century Japan. According to ancient legend, knowledge of the art was given as a divine gift to a Japanese man named Jiyemon Hiroba in 1151, to reward him for his devotion at the Katsuga shrine.

Some who doubt this legend believe that marbling was discovered purely by chance one day by a member of the Japanese imperial family, who was involved in the ancient Japanese pastime of submerging sumi ink drawings in water and watching the inks float to the top in a fleeting, yet entertaining, design. This first marbler (possibly Jiyemon) discovered that if he placed a dry piece of paper on top of the floating inks he could lift off and preserve the delicate image. His technique came to be called *suminagashi*, a Japanese word meaning "ink floating."

The subtle, flowing designs of suminagashi delighted Japan's royal household, which used the papers for poetry and calligraphy. The new art was declared off-limits to the public, and for four hundred years suminagashi remained the exclusive property of the Imperial Household and Japan's nobility. It wasn't until 1585, when Toyotomi Hideyoshi became ruler of Japan, that the general public was allowed the use of suminagashi.

A more controlled type of marbling, called *Ebru* (a Turkish word meaning "cloud art"), originated in Turkey, Persia, and India in the fifteenth century. Because Turkish marblers floated colors on a thickened water (similar to a marbling solution used today), the paints didn't wander as they did on plain water. Detailed combed patterns could be made, as well as flowing designs.

A traditional suminagashi-marbled design

Examples of marbling from this period survive to show that it was used for calligraphy and to create borders and frames for manuscripts, drawings, and paintings. Elaborate paintings of silhouetted figures were also made by applying successive resists and stencils to papers as they were marbled.

During the sixteenth century, knowledge of marbling spread slowly westward along the trade routes to Europe. By the seventeenth century, marbled papers had been seen in France, Germany, Holland, England, and Italy. Only a handful of people knew how to create the papers, however, and they were reluctant to share their knowledge. A few master marblers, using secret formulas, invented patterns and named them after the countries in which they resided. French Curl, Old Dutch, Spanish, and Italian Hair Vein are a few of the historic pattern names still in use today.

The beautiful decorative papers were prized by bookbinders; to keep up with the demand, master marblers set up guilds and workshops where young male apprentices were hired to help with production. Each apprentice was only taught a single step in the marbling process, and many were forced to work behind wooden partitions so they couldn't see what other workers were doing. A color grinder, for instance, never saw the recipe for making the marbling solution and certainly never got a chance to execute a marbled pattern. A shroud of secrecy prevailed over the new art, and the masters were content knowing that their workers could never make their own marbled sheets and set themselves up as competitors.

English bookbinders, who lusted after the marbled papers but had no idea how to make them, imported papers from the Dutch and Germans in the 1600s. To avoid paying excessive duties, the crafty Dutch often shipped marbled papers to the English by wrapping them around toys being exported to England. The unfortunate English bookbinders spent much time ironing out wrinkled papers before they could use them as endpapers in their books.

The veil of secrecy was finally lifted in 1853 when a self-taught English marbler, Charles Woolnough, described the entire marbling process in his book *The Art of Marbling*.

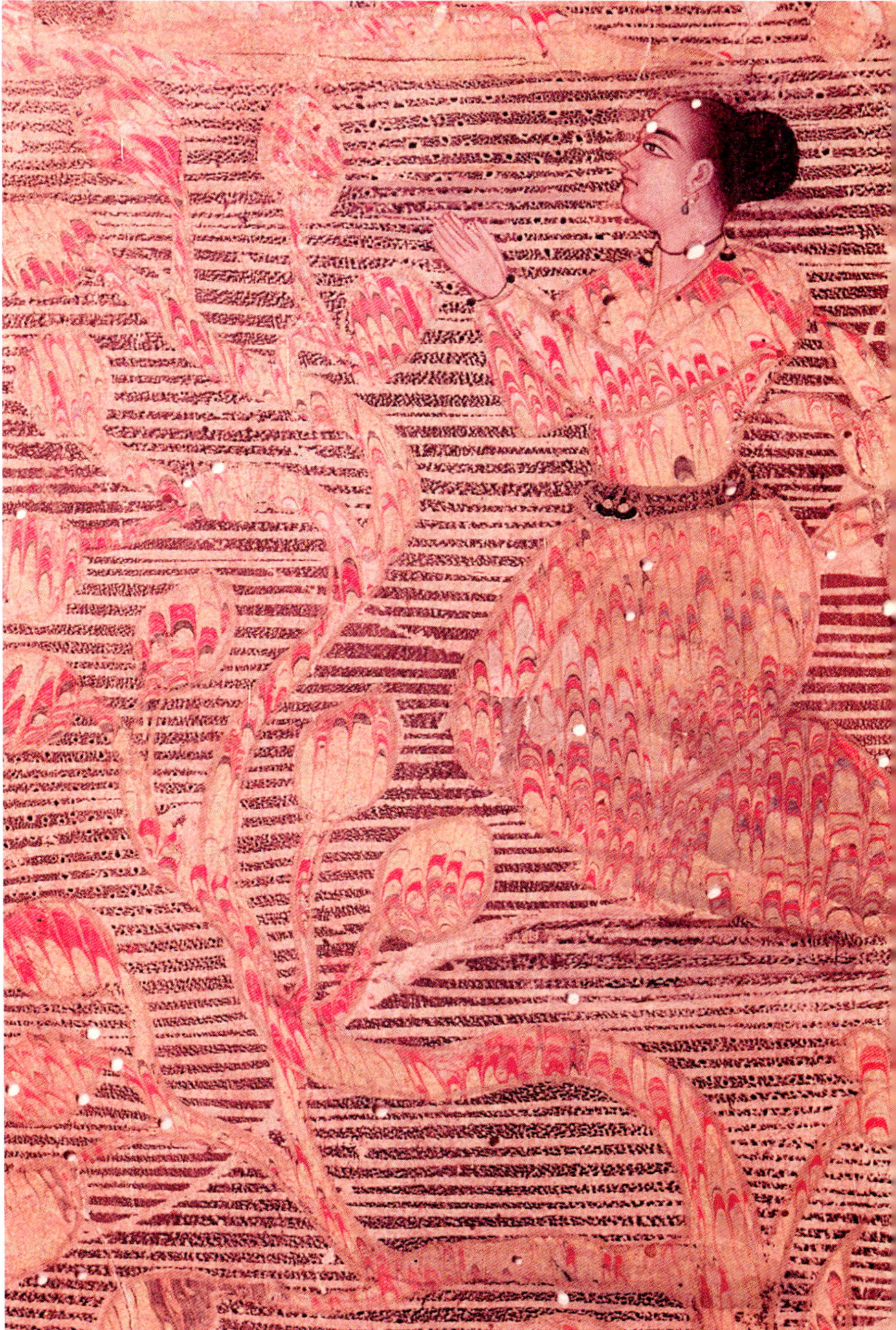

"A Female Devotee in Prayer," collection of Edwin Binney III. This marbled painting, created in India during the seventeenth century, was once thought to be a collage of cut marbled papers. Christopher Weimann's research (see page 112) revealed that it was actually a marbled painting created with a complicated series of stencils.

Although most marblers were outraged that such a textbook had been written, Woolnough was confident of his own mastery of the craft and undaunted by the prospect of competition.

Woolnough's writing remained the leading text on the craft of marbling until 1885, when Josef Halfer of Budapest published his famous book, *Die Fortschritte der Marmorierkunst.* Halfer's work, published in the United States as *The Progress of the Marbling Art,* simplified and redefined the marbling process. The book was translated into several languages and spurred the growth of marbling in Europe and America.

Unfortunately, by the time the bookbinders found themselves in possession of the coveted recipes and directions for producing marbled papers, the face of book production had changed. Binding machines had been invented and production volume was deemed much more important than fine craftsmanship. Handbinders and paper marblers, who found themselves with few orders, had to turn to other means of employment. For years, marbling lingered as an obscure book art.

It wasn't until the 1970s, when a renewed interest in calligraphy, crafts, and handmade books arose, that an interest in marbling was revived. Today, the craft is flourishing. Its modern-day masters, who probably number in the thousands, are exploring and recreating historical patterned papers, while continuing to push the limits of the medium in novel ways. Although some of the working methods and materials used today remain similar to those used hundreds of years ago, one thing is changing: the veil of secrecy is slowly being replaced by a welcome sharing of ideas and information.

Modern marblers use many of the same techniques depicted in this illustration of a seventeenth-century marbling shop. Electric blenders, of course, have made it much easier to prepare marbling solutions. And commercially prepared paints now make it unnecessary to grind marbling pigments, although some marblers still prefer to grind their own. (From A Diderot Pictorial Encyclopedia of Trades and Industry, *ed. by Charles C. Gillespie. New York: Dover Publications, 1959.)*

An experimental work by Paul Maurer. This image was created by floating airbrush inks on water.

"Where All This Is Leading To" by Susan Pogány, 24 x 18 inches (61 x 45.7 cm). A double-image watercolor-marbled work.

"The Kingdom of Rumi" by Tom Leech, 24 x 18 inches (61 x 45.7 cm). A multiple-image acrylic-marbled design with latex friskets.

1

SUMINAGASHI MARBLING

SUMINAGASHI, a Japanese word meaning "ink floating," is the oldest form of marbling. It was practiced by members of Japan's royal household more than 800 years ago. Some research suggests that suminagashi may have originated in China even earlier, before finding its way to Japan. Wherever its actual point of origin, we can be sure that suminagashi comes to us via the Orient. It brings with it a simplicity and subtle beauty that is the hallmark of many Eastern crafts, such as calligraphy and papermaking. Suminagashi also engages the oriental notion of relinquishing control over a medium, thus allowing the artist to experience, rather than manipulate, the medium. This happens naturally when working on plain water, which is set in motion by the slightest breeze or vibration.

In suminagashi, tapered brushes are used to place dots of ink and a clear solution on the surface of water to form concentric rings of color. The floating rings are then fanned or gently blown into a design. An absorbent paper is placed on top of the floating colors to create a contact print.

Although the traditional colors used for suminagashi in Japan are black, indigo (blue), and red, western marblers use many different colors, individually and in combination, to create quite vibrant papers. Patterns can range from a few simple meandering lines of color to jagged lines created by depositing hundreds of rings and then rapidly fanning them to set them in motion.

Suminagashi is a great place to begin your marbling adventures. It's the simplest type of marbling and will allow you to produce beautiful papers (and fabrics) with very little effort. Also, the gentle rhythm that results from repeatedly touching the brushes to the water's surface has a calming, almost meditative effect on most marblers.

Double-image suminagashi marbling by the author. Vibrant colors are often used by American marblers to create suminagashi designs.

Single-image suminagashi marbling

Materials

To explore basic suminagashi marbling, you'll need the following materials and equipment:

- *Marbling tray.* A photo tray, kitty litter pan, marbling tray, or similar tray about 2 inches (5.1 cm) deep and slightly larger than the paper you plan to marble, will work for suminagashi marbling. You can try using a baking pan, but many baking pans have a coating on them that can make colors sink. (This problem is usually rectified by slipping the pan inside a plastic garbage bag before filling it with water.)

  You can also build your own professional marbling tray. To build a small 13½- x 23-inch (34.3- x 58.4-cm) marbling tray with a rinsing and drainage area, cut the following pieces out of lightweight ¼-inch (6-mm) plywood:

  Two 13½- x 23-inch (34.3- x 58.4-cm) pieces, one for the base and one for the cover/rinse board (cut with a "V" and notched, as shown)

  Two 1¾- x 23-inch (4.4- x 58.4-cm) pieces for the long sides of the tray

  Three 1¾- x 13-inch (4.4- x 58.4-cm) pieces, two for the short sides and one for the drain partition (with one long edge cut at a 45 degree angle)

  One 2- x 12¾-inch (5.1- x 32.4-cm) piece for a skim board (optional, but useful in oil and watercolor marbling; see pages 35 and 63)

  Two ¼- x ¼- x 18¾-inch (0.6- x 0.6- x 47.6-cm) edge strips for the rinse board

  Drill a ¾-inch (1.9-cm) hole in one corner of the base. Sand all of the wood pieces smooth. Glue and clamp the tray edges together, then glue the rinse board strips in place. (If modifying these instructions to build a larger tray, reinforce the tray corners and edges of the drain partition with brass screws.) Paint the bottom of the tray white and waterproof the entire tray with two coats of Zip Guard Urethane.

- *Water.* You will need enough water to fill the marbling tray to a depth of 1½ inches (3.8 cm). Tap water should be fine. I've taught suminagashi workshops around the country and have never found any water to cause problems (although the water in Philadelphia, Pennsylvania seemed to make colors brighter!). If you do have problems or

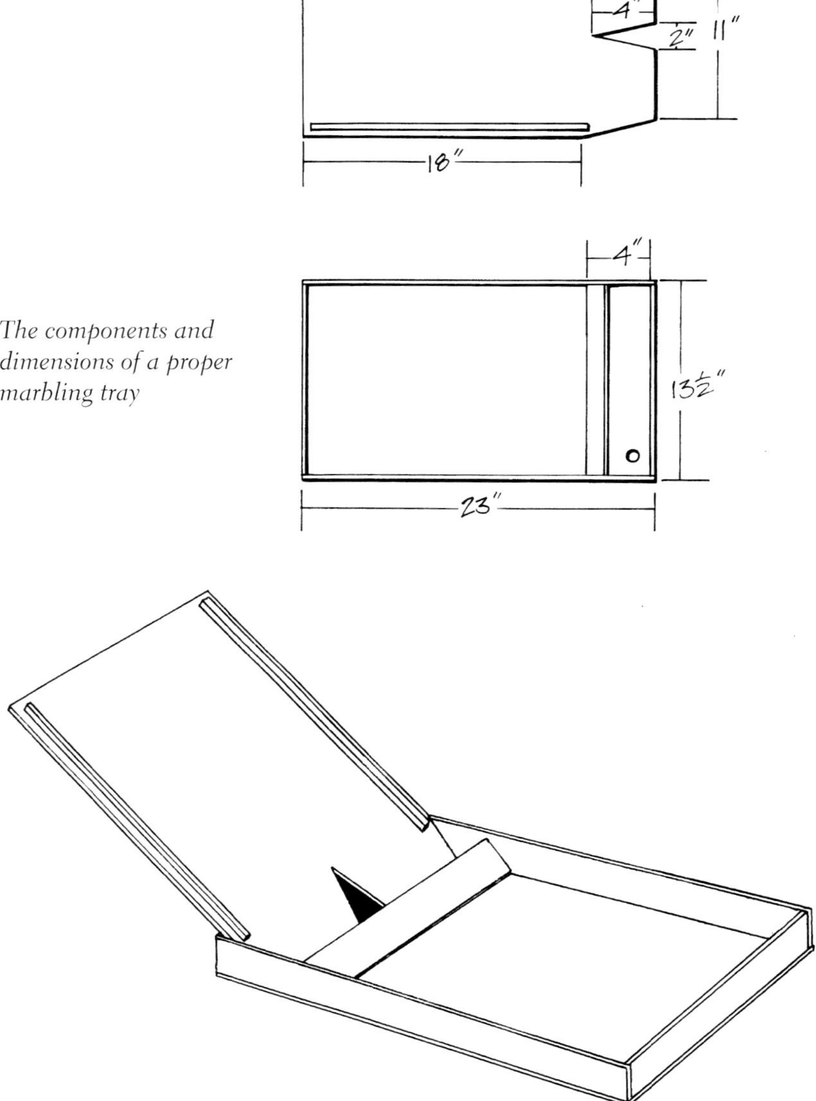

The components and dimensions of a proper marbling tray

Some of the materials and equipment used to create suminagashi-marbled designs. The fan is not essential, but is useful for making images containing traditional jagged lines.

know that your water contains many chemicals, you may want to work with bottled spring water or distilled water.

- *Colors.* Cake and liquid sumi inks, like Boku Undo colors, work well. Many drawing inks, such as Pelikan and Speedball, can also be used. The pigmented varieties will give the richest color. If you don't mind grinding ink sticks and preparing Chinese pigment chips, these can be added to your color stocks.
- *Photo-Flo 200.* Manufactured by Kodak, this surfactant (a substance that decreases the surface tension of water) is added to some brands of ink or paint (such as Boku Undo inks) to help them float and spread on the surface of water. In addition, a dispersant solution can be made by mixing one drop of Photo-Flo to 1 teaspoon (5 ml) of water. This solution acts as a kind of invisible color, pushing each dot of color it touches into a large narrow ring. It can also be used to preserve open areas in a design.
- *Color containers.* A shallow watercolor mixing tray that holds about 1 teaspoon (5 ml) of color is ideal for suminagashi marbling, although an ice cube tray can be used as a substitute. Individual lotus bowls, which have openings to use as brush rests, can also be used to hold colors. They take up a bit more space on your worktable, but will help keep your colors from accidently mixing (as they might if you get too exuberant near the watercolor mixing tray).
- *Eyedroppers.* These are used to transfer color from the original containers into your mixing tray.

- *Brushes.* Inexpensive bamboo watercolor brushes, like those made by Robert Simmons (#3 or #4 size), are needed to apply inks to the water. Brush bristles should be about 1 inch (2.5 cm) long and tapered to a point. You'll need at least four brushes.
- *Brush rest (optional).* An inexpensive plastic brush rest can be very helpful. (You won't need this if you place your inks in lotus bowls.)
- *Paper.* Absorbent papers are the most suitable for suminagashi marbling. Japanese papers such as Kozo, Moriki, and Okawara, as well as Loew-Cornell's Oriental Rice Paper Pads and Speedball block-printing paper, all marble well. Sundance Bright White Felt by the Simpson paper company is a recycled and inexpensive alternative. Handmade papers and coffee filters can also be used. Canson Mi-Teintes papers and some typing papers with a high cotton content will pick up an image, although it may be pale (which is perfect for stationery). Experiment with various papers to find your favorite. (If you alum them first, as explained in the chapter on watercolor marbling [see pages 63–64], many nonabsorbent papers can also be used.)
- *Newspapers.* Newspapers help protect tabletops and, when cut into strips 2 inches (5.1 cm) wide and a few inches longer than the width of your tray, can be used as "skim strips" to skim off excess color that remains on your water after a print is made. (A paper cutter is ideal for cutting such strips. It leaves less paper dust than the alternative: cutting with scissors or a mat knife and metal ruler.)
- *Wastebasket for wet skim strips.*
- *Paper towels.* These are useful for drawing excess water out of brushes.
- *Hand protection.* Thin latex surgical gloves or barrier hand cream can be used to keep your hands free of color.
- *Rinsing equipment.* A drain bucket and water jug will be needed to rinse papers that don't absorb all the color.
- *Rinsing support.* If you use a makeshift tray without a rinsing area and your paper has excess color that needs to be rinsed off, you'll need some sort of support to carry the wet sheet to a sink or nearby hose. Either a cookie sheet or piece of Plexiglas can be used.
- *Drying equipment.* Although drying racks designed for clothes can be used to hold wet papers, the ideal setup for drying marbled sheets is lengths of 2-inch (5.1-cm) PVC pipe strung over a clothesline. This allows the papers to dry relatively wrinkle-free without the crimps thin rods or lines can cause. If papers are sturdy, you can also hang them from a line by clipping them in place with clothespins. Try to dry papers away from a heat source, which may cause them to cockle or pucker.
- *Iron.* An iron can be used on the unmarbled sides of dry papers to remove any persistent wrinkles.
- *Soda straw and folding fan (optional).* These can be used to blow or fan floating colors into designs.

Additional materials used for experimental work will be mentioned later in this chapter.

Basic Techniques

SKIMMING

Before you begin marbling, you'll need to skim off dust that has settled on the water in your tray. You'll also need to skim off any excess color that remains in your tray between prints. To skim, just drag a 2-inch-wide (5.1-cm-wide) strip of newspaper (a "skim strip") across the water's surface, gathering up debris or color until you can bring it up and out of the tray. (If your tray has no drainage area, place some newspaper on the worktable at the end of the tray to receive the refuse.) As you pull the skim strip toward you, turn its front edge up slightly and make sure that the sides of the strip slide against the edge of the marbling tray. This will prevent excess color from escaping around the edges of the skim strip.

Skimming is especially important when using drawing inks. Their residue will often prevent other colors from floating. If conditions get really dirty, you can, of course, just refill your tray with clean water. (Note: Try to marble paper that is only slightly smaller than the dimensions of the marbling tray. This way, most of the color will be deposited on the sheet and less skimming will be necessary.)

To skim off dust before applying the suminagashi colors, hold the newspaper strip as shown and pull it down the length of the tray. Use the same technique to remove excess color that remains after a print is made.

TESTING THE COLOR

For successful suminagashi marbling, inks must disperse over the surface of the water in your tray. To determine whether the color you're using will disperse properly, transfer 1 teaspoon (5 ml) of color into your mixing tray or lotus bowl. Dip your brush into the color, wipe off any excess, and repoint your brush by drawing it across the edge of the container. Touch the tip of the brush to the surface of the water in your tray—the color should rapidly spread into a circle about 3 inches (7.6 cm) in diameter. If the color doesn't spread, or if it sinks, stir a single drop of Photo-Flo into the color in the mixing tray and test it again. Any color that still does not float after the Photo-Flo has been added will not work for suminagashi marbling.

It's important to make sure that your mixture of color and Photo-Flo is well stirred. If it isn't, the Photo-Flo will settle out and the color will begin to sink. This may tempt you to add more Photo-Flo to your color which, ironically, will *make* the color sink. (A residue of Photo-Flo in the water will alter the water's surface tension so much that color can't push against it to float.)

APPLYING AND PATTERNING THE COLORS

Fill two sections of your mixing tray or two lotus bowls with different colored inks. Fill a third section or lotus bowl with a dispersant solution of 1 teaspoon (5 ml) water and one drop Photo-Flo. Skim the marbling tray to remove any dust and wait until the water has stopped moving. Then start by holding two brushes, one loaded with well-stirred and tested color and the other loaded only with well-stirred dispersant. Barely touch the center of the water with the color-loaded brush, releasing a drop of color. The drop should expand into a large circle of color. Now touch the center of the expanded drop of color with the tip of the dispersant brush. The dispersant solution will propel the circle of color into a large ring.

Alternately apply color and dispersant until a number of concentric clear and colored rings are formed. Then gently blow the rings into a design. If you blow from the side of the tray, the lines of color will be more meandering as they slowly flow in and around each other. A soda straw can be used to direct air and propel specific parts of the floating rings. Because the colors are floating on water, even tapping the tray or bumping your worktable will cause the colors to move in response to the vibration. A breeze from an open window, nearby fan, or air conditioner will also affect patterning and may be considered either a help or hindrance to your work. To produce a pattern with sharp angular lines, lean over the floating colors and blow sharply down on them. To create a more jagged pattern, fan the colors rapidly from above with a piece of cardboard or a handheld fan.

Alternately apply color and dispersant to build up a number of concentric color rings.

Fan the floating rings of color or blow sharply down on them to create the jagged lines seen in traditional suminagashi marbling.

Deposit color more quickly by learning to hold two color brushes in one hand and the dispersant brush in the other.

Japanese suminagashi masters traditionally applied inks to water by holding two color-loaded brushes in one hand and a brush charged with dispersant (a pine oil) in the other, depositing between fifty and one hundred rings before patterning them. Once you're comfortable applying color and dispersant with two brushes, try working with three, just as the Japanese masters did.

Work in as many colors as you wish, creating concentric rings by alternating color with dispersant or by applying one color on top of another without using dispersant. Work in the center of the tray to build up a large bull's-eye, or deposit smaller circles of color in various sections of the tray to create other interesting designs.

To lessen color sinkage, remember to apply your colors gently instead of flinging them down into the water. Also, if you let the color flow from the tip of the brush, and are careful not to dunk the brush, you won't run the risk of diluting your colors by returning a water-soaked brush to them.

Be aware that as long as you let your brush remain in contact with the water, either dispersant or color will flow from it, creating an ever wider colored or clear ring. This can be helpful for varying the size of your rings and giving you more patterning options, but it also means that your brush can fill with water, which will then dilute the color in your mixing tray when you reload your brush. If you think your brush has drawn water back up into it, touch it to a paper towel to remove the water.

MAKING THE PRINT

When you have finished applying and patterning the colors, gently lay a sheet of absorbent paper on top of the water to make a contact print. Be careful not to shift the paper or flop it down as you will disturb the design and possibly trap air beneath the paper, creating an unsightly void in the pattern.

One way to apply the paper is to hold it by diagonal corners so that it droops in the center. Steady one hand on the far corner of the tray and, while continuing to hold the paper, ease the far edge onto the color. Then, in one fluid motion, lower the rest of the sheet onto the floating pattern. If you're marbling very thin sheets of paper, leave the near edge of the sheet dry so you can pick the paper up without tearing it.

The paper will absorb the inks immediately upon contact. Remove the sheet by picking up the edges farthest away from you and then peeling it back onto the rinse board or paper support. (Sprinkle a few drops of water on the support if it's dry to keep the first piece of marbled paper from sliding down.)

RINSING AND DRYING

If you notice an excess of color running from the marbled paper, or if you're using black ink (which has the nasty habit of developing a smoky haze), you should rinse the sheet. Gently pour water over it, starting at the top, until the water runs off clear. If you're using a marbling tray with a drain hole in the bottom, excess water can conveniently run off into a waiting bucket.

If you're marbling a thin sheet and have left one edge dry for safer handling, or if you're confident there's no excess color that may later bleed, you can pick up the sheet by the edge closest to you and carry it directly to the drying area.

Once your sheets have dried, you can flatten them by placing them under books or a board overnight. Sheets may also be pressed on their unmarbled sides with a warm iron.

(Note: When finished marbling, be sure to clean trays, brushes, and color containers with water only, as any soap residue [a surfactant] will cause problems in your next marbling session.)

Make the print by steadying one hand on the far corner of the marbling tray and easing the far paper edge onto the color. Hold that edge steady while you lower the rest of the sheet.

Rinse the paper to remove any excess color. A divided marbling tray will support the rinse board and make this process easy.

Altering the Image with Advanced Techniques

OTHER PATTERNING OPTIONS

Because the suminagashi colors are floated on plain water, they will sink if you try to manipulate them with marbling combs or rakes. Even using a simple stylus (a hard-pointed pen-shaped instrument) will often disturb colors enough to sink them or send them rushing out of control.

To devise a simple tool that gently patterns the suminagashi colors, tape a single cat whisker to the wrong end of a paint brush. (A single human hair can be substituted if you don't have a cat or can't find any stray whiskers.) Pull the hair or kitty-whisker brush in a gentle back-and-forth motion horizontally through the rings of color to create delicate designs.

You can also pattern colors by gently blowing through a soda straw or rubber tube to manipulate specific parts of a design. To further alter the design, apply color or alcohol to a toothbrush and spatter it over the floating color by dragging your finger toward you over the brush bristles.

You can compress, distort, or create holes in rings of color by touching them with a brush or toothpick dipped in a weak solution of Photo-Flo and water. A toothpick can also be used to apply spots of color for additional design options.

These results were achieved by dragging a cat whisker, taped to the wrong end of a paint brush, through rings of color. This type of patterning will be easier if you work with a minimum amount of water in your tray to decrease pattern movement.

Select areas of this marbled design were compressed by touching them with the dispersant brush.

OVERMARBLING

After a marbled paper has dried, it can often be marbled a second time to produce an overmarbled or "ghost" print. (Unfortunately, some prints made with shellac-based inks repel a second coat of color and can't be successfully overmarbled.) The intersecting lines created by overmarbling form new patterns and colors that can save a previously uninteresting print.

Many successful overmarbled prints begin with an uncomplicated base print of wide, meandering bands of color. When a second coat of thinner, more jagged lines (the result of fanning the colors) is applied, both layers can clearly be seen, creating interest in the work without making it too busy. If the second coat is created with colors that are shades of the primary image, success is practically guaranteed. Some overmarbled sheets with three layers of primary and secondary colors have an amazing brilliance.

Before you overmarble a dried sheet, flatten it completely by ironing its unmarbled side. Wrinkles or cockled areas in the sheet can create air pockets, which can lead to voids in the remarbled image.

USING FRISKETS

A frisket is a masking device that can be used to preserve an area within a marbled pattern. Floating paper friskets, frisket film, liquid frisket, and even gummed labels can be used to preserve blank areas to show the paper color or, if you're overmarbling, to preserve areas of the marbled underpainting. Because the clear rings between colors usually don't work well with frisket work, it's best to alternate colored rings to create the background for these designs.

This overmarbled design was created by varying the amount of dispersant applied between colored rings and the amount of time the brush was allowed to release color.

FLOATING FRISKETS

To create a floating frisket, cut a geometric pattern or simple design out of lightweight paper. Float the frisket on top of patterned suminagashi colors and then apply the paper you want to marble. Results may be unpredictable and, for this technique to work, you need to move quickly. The sheet to be marbled must be laid down before the floating paper frisket begins to curl or sink. A student in one of my marbling classes had a fine time cutting designs in coffee filters and using them as floating friskets. Because she worked quickly (before the filters sank), results were good. Leaves, too, can be floated atop the colors as simple friskets.

FRISKET FILM

For more professional results, try making friskets with frisket film. It comes in sheets and rolls and, although more expensive than plain paper, will help you avoid the fuzzy edges that sometimes result when color leaks under a floating frisket. When choosing frisket film, be sure to use a low-tack variety that won't damage the soft paper when removed. In fact, it's best to test a bit of the film on the paper you intend to marble to make sure it won't cause problems. Contact paper may also be used as frisket material with good results, although it may resist sticking in very humid conditions.

Simple designs can be cut out of frisket film with scissors. More complicated designs can be drawn, rubber-stamped, or traced on the film and then cut out with a swivel or X-acto knife. (Be sure to cut over a self-healing mat or piece of glass with taped edges.) You can use either the positive images (birds, for example) or the negative image (the film showing the outline of several birds) to create the frisket.

After you've cut out your design and removed it from the paper backing, use a bone folder (a dull pointed tool) to burnish the frisket film or contact paper in place on your sheet. Pattern your colors and then carefully apply the sheet. Remove the marbled sheet to your drain board and rinse it to remove any excess color. Gently peel off the frisket while the sheet is still damp.

LIQUID FRISKET

Liquid frisket, available at art supply stores, can be used to paint or letter directly on a sheet of paper. The brush or pen strokes will be faithfully reproduced when the mask is removed. Liquid frisket can also be diluted and dripped or splattered on a sheet of paper to create abstract designs.

To use liquid frisket, apply it with a brush or pen and let it dry fully before marbling the sheet. Rinse the paper and, when the paper has *completely* dried, gently peel off the liquid frisket.

After cutting out the design and removing the frisket film from its backing, burnish the frisket in place on the sheet to be marbled. Friskets can be used on a blank sheet of paper, or to preserve some of the pattern from a previously marbled design.

Gently peel frisket film from the marbled sheet while the sheet is still damp to minimize damage to the paper.

CREATING FRACTURED AND UNUSUAL DESIGNS

When working in extremely hot and dry conditions, inks that previously behaved quite normally can suddenly begin forming rings that alternately break up into segments or begin twisting and turning erratically. Even Boku Undo inks, which are normally quite predictable, can take on a new personality, especially if you're working in sunlight or under an overhead fan. Sometimes pollution in the marbling tray, the result of not skimming well, can also lead to strange designs.

Inks with a shellac base (difficult to find these days) will often dry on the surface of the water and break up. The chemistry of other inks, like Higgins and Speedball waterproof inks and some airbrush colors, will react together in dry conditions to form star shapes, mosslike textures, or chunks of color that break off from the rest of the design like floating icebergs. Sometimes the inks dry so completely on the surface of the water that they form a hard, icelike film that actually fractures into pieces when you touch it with a toothpick.

Boku Undo inks can be forced into a segmented design if, after applying them in rings, you touch them with a bit of turpentine and then add a few drops of turpentine to the water in the tray. Cosmetic lotions with a high oil content can also create strange reactions if added to the colors or water as you marble.

Carol McNally, a marbler well grounded in chemistry, has discovered a method of working with Higgins Waterproof Drawing Ink that she uses to create interesting designs (see opposite, below right). Although not all Higgins colors react this way, the black (#4415) and, to a lesser degree, the blue (#4145) will usually cooperate. (I mixed the black and blue together with good results.)

Carol's technique is as follows: Add 1 tablespoon (15 ml) of white vinegar to 1 gallon (3.8 l) of water. Pour the mixture into your tray. Block off two-thirds of the water's surface with paper strips, leaving the center of the tray open. Using a toothpick, apply successive dots of one color in the center of the tray until the color is very dense. Then gently pull each strip of paper toward the tray's edge before picking it up and out of the tray. As the paper is pulled away, it stretches the color and the ink separates into mossy, fibrous rings. Make a print by laying your paper on top of the color, and rinse as usual.

Tray pollution and extremely dry conditions helped Paul Maurer create this segmented suminagashi design.

This design, which resembles broken pottery, resulted when Higgins ink was applied over concentric rings of Speedball inks.

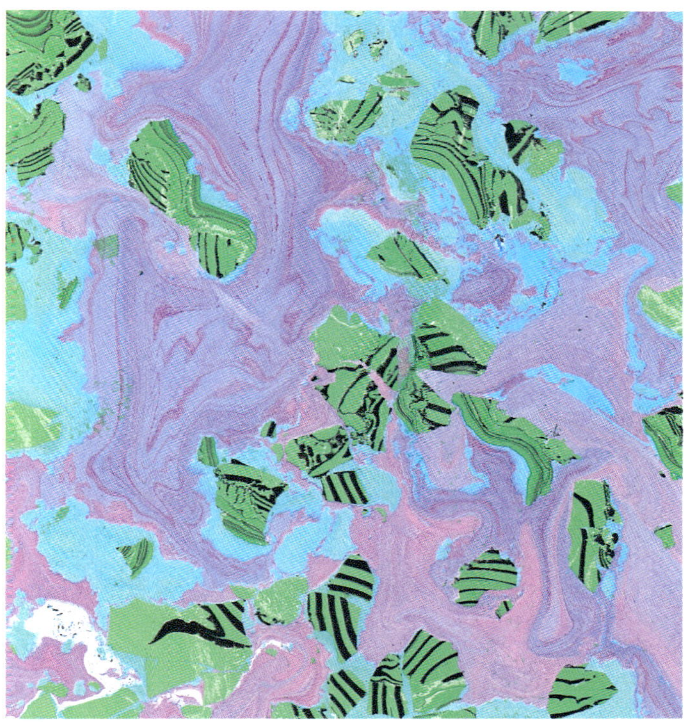

In this design, airbrush colors applied over Higgins ink produced blocks of color that floated off like icebergs.

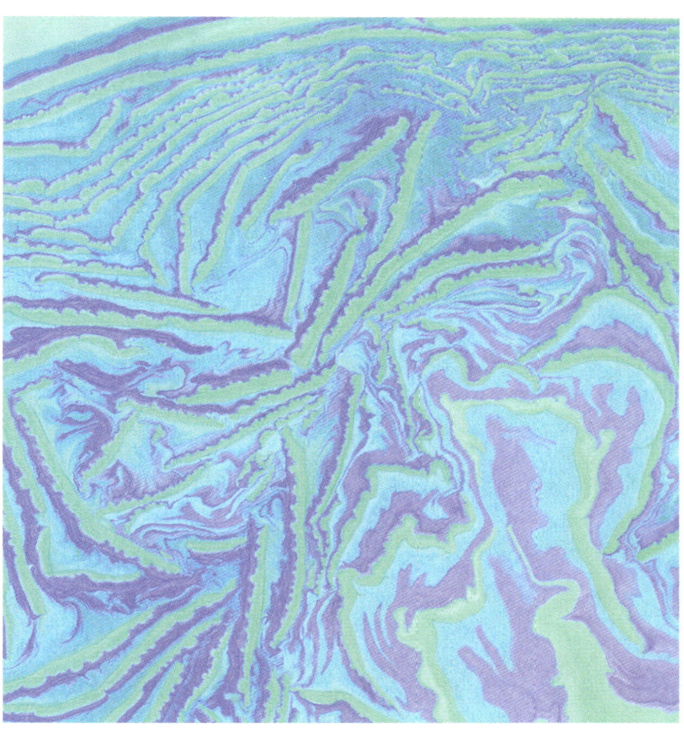

When allowed to sit on the water for several minutes, Golden airbrush colors began to break out of their ringed formation to form segmented curved shapes.

When Boku Undo colors and black Higgins ink were applied in rings in several sections of the tray, they at first seemed to be compatible. After a minute or two, however, the Higgins black ink began breaking up and creating unusual shapes.

"Dark Bloom," from the Cricket Moon Series by Carol McNally, 14⅜ x 10¾ inches (36.5 x 27.3 cm). Carol uses Higgins black ink and a novel type of paper manipulation to pull the inks into a design.

TROUBLESHOOTING

Although suminagashi marbling is the least trouble-laden of all the types of marbling, problems do sometimes arise. Common problems and their possible causes and solutions are listed below.

Colors sink when applied.

1. The color may need surfactant to spread and float. Stir a single drop of surfactant (Photo-Flo) into the container of color.
2. You may not have stirred the surfactant into the color. Be sure to stir the color each time you apply it.
3. You may have added too much surfactant to the color and it mixed into the water, changing the surface tension so much that the inks can no longer spread and float. Start over with fresh ink and fresh water in the tray. If your color needs surfactant, add only one drop of Photo-Flo for each teaspoon of color and stir well before testing it on the water.
4. You may be loading too much ink on the brush. Next time, wipe your brush against the side of the color container to remove some ink before applying the brush to the water.
5. You may be applying color too heavy-handedly. Just "kiss" the surface of the water instead of flinging the color off your brush.

Colors don't spread enough when they're applied.

1. See the first three entries above.
2. If you've deposited many rings of color in your tray, the surface tension may have built up so much that it will not allow you to deposit more color. It's time to print!
3. The water in your tray may be too dirty, which can impede your color spread. Pour out the water and refill your tray.

Colors become pale.

1. Your brush may be absorbing water when you apply the color, which is then diluting the color in your mixing tray when you reload the brush. Wipe your brushes on a paper towel to draw out the moisture and start over with fresh color. When applying the color, be sure to just touch the surface of the water instead of dunking your brush. If you continue to have trouble, wipe your brush against a paper towel to remove the water each time you deposit color.
2. You may have added too much surfactant to the colors. This will cause them to expand and grow pale at first. (Later, the colors will sink.)

Colors break up into weird shapes and segmented lines (see A, opposite top)

1. A polluted tray may be the culprit. Before replacing your water, however, try marbling a few sheets like this on purpose. Some of these "funky" papers are actually quite interesting and are impossible to duplicate. When you've had enough, replace the dirty water in your tray with clean water.
2. The space you are working in may be too dry, hot, sunny, or breezy. Try increasing the level of humidity in your workspace by using a humidifier, and avoid hot halogen lights, overhead fans, and direct sunlight. All of these can cause colors to dry and break up on the surface of the water.

Colors wash off when the marbled print is rinsed.

Slight color bleed is normal when you've built up a high concentration of color in the tray, especially when working with a lot of black ink. If *most* of the color washes off a sheet, however, you may be using a nonporous paper or a paper too heavily sized or coated. Choose a softer Japanese paper instead.

White spots appear on the marbled print (see B, below right).

1. Small white spots may be the result of dust or debris that wasn't skimmed off before you began applying colors.
2. Large white spots are probably the result of air being trapped between the paper and the surface of the water. Try to maintain the paper's natural flexibility as you roll it down onto the patterned water. If you apply the paper as though it is a rigid board, you will cause an air bubble to form and prevent color from adhering. (You can usually patch an area by tapping against the bubble through the back of your paper, but the flaw will still be visible in the finished sheet.)

Long white streaks or lines appear on the marbled print (see B, right).
These lines or interruptions in a pattern (sometimes called "hesitation marks" or "shift marks") are the result of not applying the paper properly. Two common ways of misapplying the paper are:

1. You may have moved the paper erratically while applying it to your floating pattern. This may have prewetted an area and prevented it from absorbing color.
2. You may have flopped the end of the paper down when applying it to your floating pattern. Be sure to hold on to both ends of the paper until it has made complete contact with the color.

Short lines that look like pulls or runs appear on the marbled print (see C, right)
These odd little pattern interruptions result when colors are applied very rapidly. Sometimes the brush movement causes a tiny droplet of water to splash up and travel across the paper for a short distance, bisecting a nearby line of color. This is fun to watch and usually only happens to confident marblers. The only remedy is to slow down (or to try to perfect this as a patterning variation).

A. Convoluted and segmented lines

B. An air-bubble void and hesitation mark

C. Short pattern interruptions

2

OIL COLOR MARBLING

OIL-MARBLED PAPERS have a bold richness that is quite a counterbalance to the delicacy of suminagashi designs. Once you've seen this type of marbling, with its vibrant swirls of color and dappled areas with tiny beads of reticulated paint, you'll easily recognize it again. Oil color marbling is unlike any other kind of marbling. Its vivid painterly quality has long been prized, and it was used extensively by eighteenth-century European artisans for the endpapers and cover papers of their handbound books.

Oil color marbling is similar to suminagashi marbling (see Chapter 1, Suminagashi Marbling) in that colors are floated on a liquid and a sheet of paper is applied to the floating colors to make a contact print. The materials and techniques used in oil color marbling, however, are quite different. In addition to being floated on water, oil marbling colors can be floated on a thickened liquid known as *marbling size*, and patterned to a limited degree, although you'll never have the control you can experience with watercolor paints (see Chapter 3, Watercolor Marbling). Oil colors tend to have their own agendas and begin patterning themselves as soon as they touch the water or marbling size. You can take your time when marbling with oil paints, and even walk away from the tray for an hour before making the print. It's fun to check in every 15 minutes or so to see what changes have taken place. Colors that look like tiny, undulating globs of paint after five minutes can metamorphose into a lacy matrix of color after half an hour.

Unfortunately, oil color marbling is messier than suminagashi marbling, and more time-consuming to clean up. Also, because many of the paints and thinners have noxious fumes, you may need to use a vapor respirator or good exhaust fan unless you're working outside. Oil marblers agree, however, that the rich textures and colors achieved with oil paints make any extra effort worthwhile.

An oil-marbled print created on a thickened marbling size by Paul Maurer. The thickened base keeps the colors from moving as rapidly as they do on water, allowing a limited degree of patterning.

This design was created by using a stylus to pattern Grumbacher MAX oil paints floating on a size.

Materials

Here's what you'll need to explore oil marbling:

- *Marbling tray.* See page 16 for more information. You can use a purchased, constructed, or makeshift tray. (Many oil marblers like to work in trays constructed of welded sheet metal, which make cleanup easier when paint thinner is used.) Whatever type of tray you use, it should be reserved for oil marbling alone. Any residue of paints or thinner on the tray or marbling tools can make suminagashi or watercolor paints sink.
- *Small 8- x 10-inch (20.3- x 25.4-cm) testing tray (optional).* More commonly used for watercolor marbling (see page 66), this type of tray allows you to test and adjust your colors without polluting the large tray.
- *Water.* Tap water usually works fine. You'll need enough to fill your tray to a depth of 1½ inches (3.8 cm).
- *Colors.* Any liquid or paste oil colors can be used. Artist's oils, lithography inks, etching inks, and printer's inks usually produce good results. Gold and silver decorator's enamels and some sign-painting paints also work. Two relatively new paints, MAX and MAX2 by Grumbacher, can be thinned and cleaned up with water, a real bonus for people who are allergic to solvents.
- *Photo-Flo 200.* A drop or two of Photo-Flo often helps problem colors spread on water or size. (Common dish detergent, another surfactant, can also be used. Experiment to find the proper dilution of your brand.)
- *Linseed oil.* Linseed oil makes colors more luminous and helps soften paste colors.
- *Mineral spirits or Safe Solve.* These solvents can be used to dilute conventional oil colors, to help disperse color, and to clean oil marbling equipment. Safe Solve is a nontoxic turpentine substitute that is safer to use than other paint thinners.
- *Color containers.* Use metal or glass containers. Plastic containers can also be used as long as they are advertised as safe for storing paints and solvents.

Some of the materials and equipment used for oil marbling

To make a whisk, bind bundles of broom straw with string or rubber bands. Then soak the whisks overnight to remove any broomcorn dust.

- *Color-stirring sticks.* Dowels, spoons, or Popsicle sticks can be used to stir colors and mix them with additives.
- *Color applicators.* Eyedroppers, pipettes, and small bamboo brushes (like those used for suminagashi marbling, see page 18) can be used to deposit color on the water or size. A "drop brush" or sign-painter's brush with soft, long bristles is the tool of choice for most professional oil marblers.

  Another important tool is the broom straw whisk. To make a whisk, purchase a natural straw broom or loose broomcorn from a marbling supply house and cut 6-inch (15.2-cm) lengths of straw from it. (Either the grassy or the stiff ends of the straw can be used.) Compress the straw into a 1-inch-wide (2.5-cm-wide) bundle and bind it with string or rubber bands, as shown above. Make several whisks—you'll need one for each color used.
- *Paper and other objects.* Special papers aren't necessary for oil color marbling. As long as a paper can withstand being wet and its surface isn't so slick that it will repel color, it can be oil marbled. Other materials, like fabric, wood, and bisque-fired clay, can also be marbled (see Chapter 4, Marbling Fabric and Other Materials). I have a friend who once made some striking but rather uncomfortable benches from oil-marbled concrete blocks.
- *Newspapers.* Newspapers are used for making skim strips to skim off excess color and dust, and for covering work areas. (See page 18 for more information about skim strips.) Paper that is oil-marbled on water can be laid on newspapers to dry. Any marbling size present on the sheets, however, can make them stick to the newspaper.
- *Skim board.* A narrow skim board, cut slightly shorter than the width of your tray, is used to remove bubbles when marbling on a thickened base or size. A thin strip of balsa wood about 2 inches (5.1 cm) wide is ideal. A piece of a wooden yardstick can also be used.
- *Patterning tools.* See page 38.
- *Paper towels.* Paper towels are used for blotting excess paint off newly marbled papers and for cleanup.
- *Rinsing equipment.* If your tray doesn't have a cover/rinse board, use a cookie sheet or piece of Plexiglas to hold your paper during rinsing. You can use a jug of water to rinse papers at your marbling tray if the tray has a section for rinsing. Otherwise, a nearby hose and bucket or utility sink can be used. Some oil marblers prefer to rinse their sheets by laying them in a separate tray of water. (If you're marbling on plain water, rinsing may not be necessary.)
- *Drying equipment.* PVC pipe strung on a clothesline makes a great support for drying papers (see page 18). If you're marbling on plain water, you can just lay marbled papers on sheets of newspaper.
- *Cleanup equipment.* A scrub brush, dish detergent, and nonchlorine powdered cleanser are needed for cleaning up. Pipe cleaners are used for cleaning eyedroppers.
- *Respirator and exhaust fan.* It's wise to wear a respirator when working around toxic paints and thinners. An exhaust fan also helps rid your studio of harmful fumes.
- *Thin vinyl gloves or oil-repellant barrier hand cream.* Either of these will protect your hands from stains and the irritating effects of solvents.

Basic Techniques

MIXING THE COLOR

If you're marbling with liquid oils, pour about ¼ cup (60 ml) of well-stirred paint into a container. Then add about one-fifth as much linseed oil and enough thinner to bring the paint to a milky consistency.

If you're working with paste oils, start by putting about 2 tablespoons (30 ml) of color into a container. Then add one-fourth as much linseed oil. Use a dowel or stick to push and stir the oil into the color until the mixture is smooth, and add a bit more linseed oil to bring the color to a creamy consistency. (If the color remains stringy or feels gritty, you may have to homogenize it with a mortar and pestle.) When the color is well creamed, stir in enough thinner to bring it to a milky consistency.

To prepare MAX oils for marbling, add a little water and stir. Then add just enough water to bring the mixture to a milky consistency.

TESTING THE COLOR

To test a color, first skim a water-filled marbling tray with a strip of newspaper to remove surface skin and dust. Then insert a whisk into a well-mixed color. Stir, and tap off any excess paint. Hold the whisk above the tray and tap it against a stick or your gloved finger to broadcast droplets of paint. The paint should float and spread, but still retain its color.

If the paint spreads so much that it becomes transparent, add more color to your mixture. If it sinks to the bottom of the tray, it's probably too thick and requires additional thinner. Test all the colors to make sure they respond correctly.

Usually, if all the colors test out individually, they'll work together in the marbling tray. Sometimes, however, a particular color alters the surface tension of the water so much that when another color follows it, it can't spread enough to float. To solve this problem, either apply the colors in a sequence that keeps them all afloat, or add more Photo-Flo or thinner to the hesitant color to help it disperse. If you find that a few colors seem hesitant to float with each other, try applying them simultaneously by tapping three whisks or shaking three brushes in unison.

Although MAX oils will produce a fine oil-marbled image, you will experience more sinkage with them than with traditional oils. This should not, however, pose a serious problem unless you're doing a demonstration and want a pristine tray bottom.

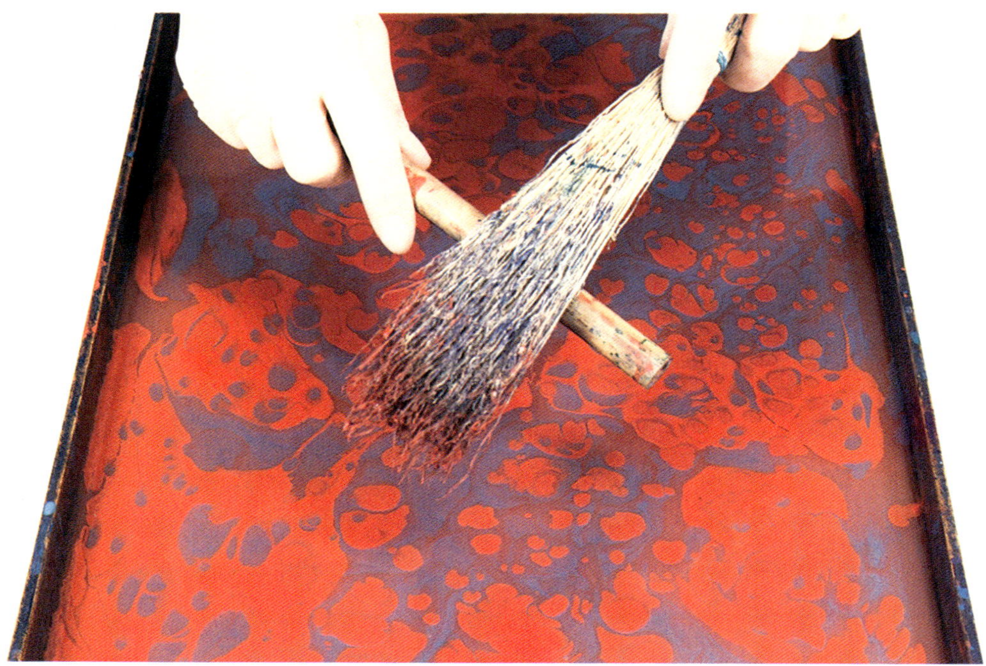

To use a whisk correctly, tap it against a stick or your gloved finger to broadcast droplets of paint.

MARBLING ON WATER

APPLYING THE COLORS

Skim the surface of the water, then apply your oil colors in various sections of the marbling tray. Use whisks, brushes, pipettes, or eyedroppers to apply the colors, remembering to first stir each color well. If you're using an eyedropper or pipette, fill it with paint and keep pressure on the bulb so you don't draw in air, which would cause you to deposit bubbles of paint on the water.

The colors you apply will begin flowing in and around each other to form designs. It may be frustrating to watch an image disappear before you can lay down a sheet of paper to capture it, but that's the nature of marbling on water—especially with oil paints, which seem to have a mind of their own.

MAKING THE PRINT

Make a print by lowering a sheet of paper onto the floating colors. Use the same technique discussed in suminagashi marbling (see page 21), working slowly and carefully to avoid trapping air bubbles beneath the sheet. When your sheet has been printed, lift it out of the marbling tray and place it on your drain board or rinse board if you're using a makeshift tray. Rinse with water and use a paper towel to blot off any excess color before carrying the sheet to your drying line or newspaper. Finally, remember to skim off excess color on your water before beginning another print.

An oil-marbled design created on water by Gabriele Grünebaum

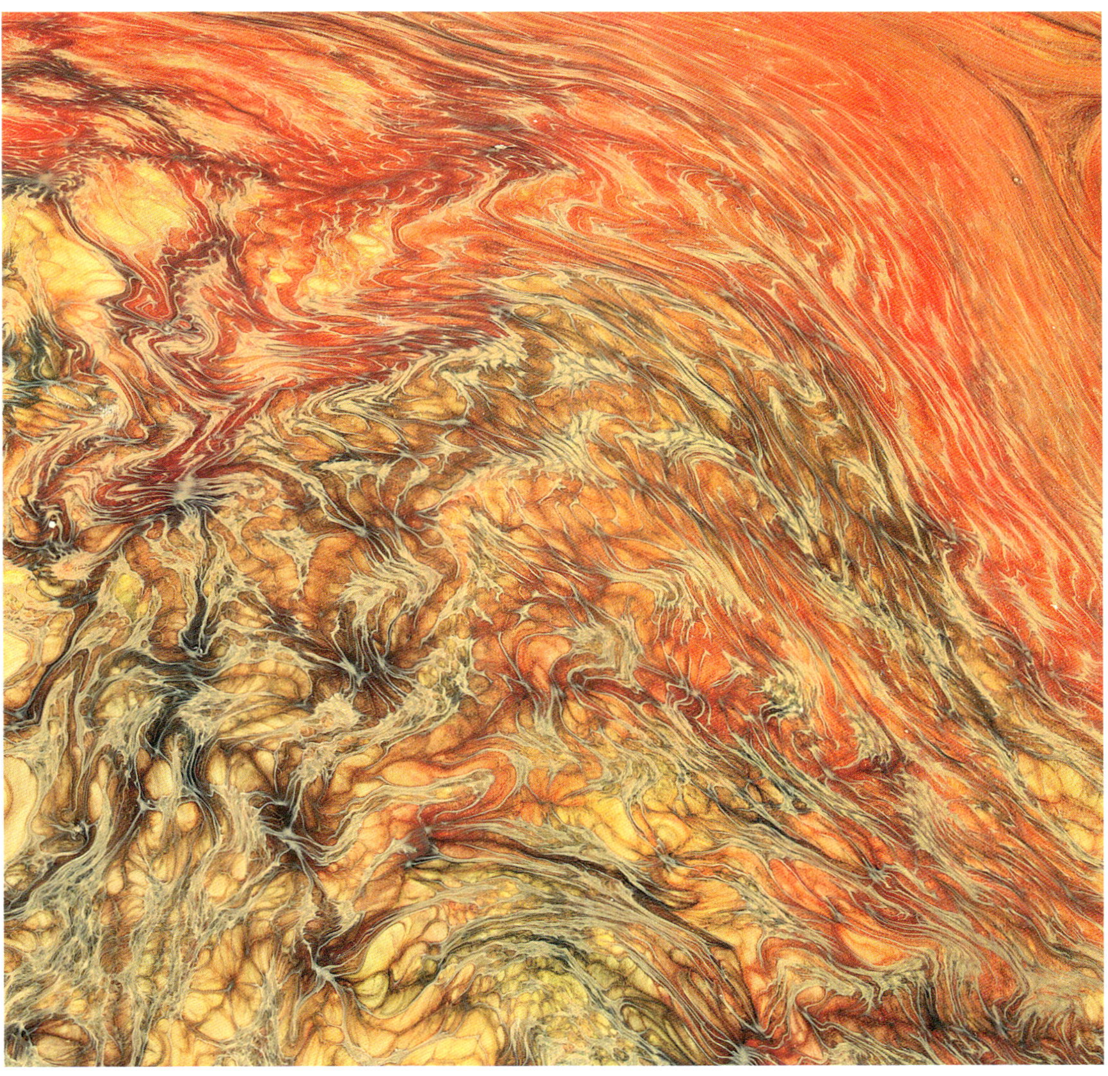

MARBLING ON A SIZE

A thickened marbling size, made by mixing water with powdered methyl cellulose or powdered *carrageenan* (an extract of Irish seaweed, available from a marbling supply house) will allow you to gain some control over the floating colors. (Other size possibilities to explore for novel effects are unflavored food gelatin and liquid starch.) Because the colors are unable to move as freely on a thicker base, you can pattern them to a limited degree.

To make carrageenan blender size, turn the blender on low and tap the powder into the moving water a little at a time.

Use a skim board to remove bubbles introduced by blending the size.

In addition to the materials and equipment noted previously, you'll need a tablespoon, a blender for mixing carrageenan size (or large pot for mixing methyl cellulose size), a 1-gallon (3.8-l) jug for dispensing rinse water, and a large rinse board and bucket or nearby sink for rinsing excess size from your marbled sheets.

MAKING A CARRAGEENAN BLENDER SIZE

Carrageenan is a nontoxic food additive used in toothpaste, ice cream, and many other products, so you can use your kitchen blender to mix up the size. The basic recipe calls for mixing 2 level tablespoons (30 g) of powdered carrageenan with 1 gallon (3.8 l) of water. Begin by figuring out the amount of size you'll need for your tray. (A small 13½- x 23-inch [34.3- x 58.4-cm] tray will use about 1 gallon [3.8 l] of size.) Measure out the proper amounts of carrageenan and water. Pour some of the water into your blender, filling it about two-thirds full, and turn the blender on low. While the water is moving, slowly tap in a little less than 1 tablespoon (15 g) of the carrageenan. Blend for several seconds to dissolve it. Then add more of the water to bring the blender to three-quarters full. Blend another minute before pouring the mixture into a waiting pot or bucket.

Repeat the steps above until you've mixed all of the water and carrageenan you'd measured out. Stir the mixture in the pot or bucket, then pour it into your tray to fill it to a depth of about 1½ inches (3.8 cm). If you let the size stand overnight, the bubbles introduced by blending will dissipate. If you want to begin marbling immediately, you'll need to remove the bubbles with a skim board before applying your colors.

MAKING A METHYL CELLULOSE SIZE

Follow the directions provided with the methyl cellulose you purchased, as some require the addition of ammonia or vinegar to dissolve properly. Then stir well and add enough water to bring the size to a milky consistency. (The recipe we use calls for 4 table-spoons [60 g] of methyl cellulose to about 6 pints [2.8 l] of water.) Let the mixture stand until it becomes clear and smooth (about 15 minutes).

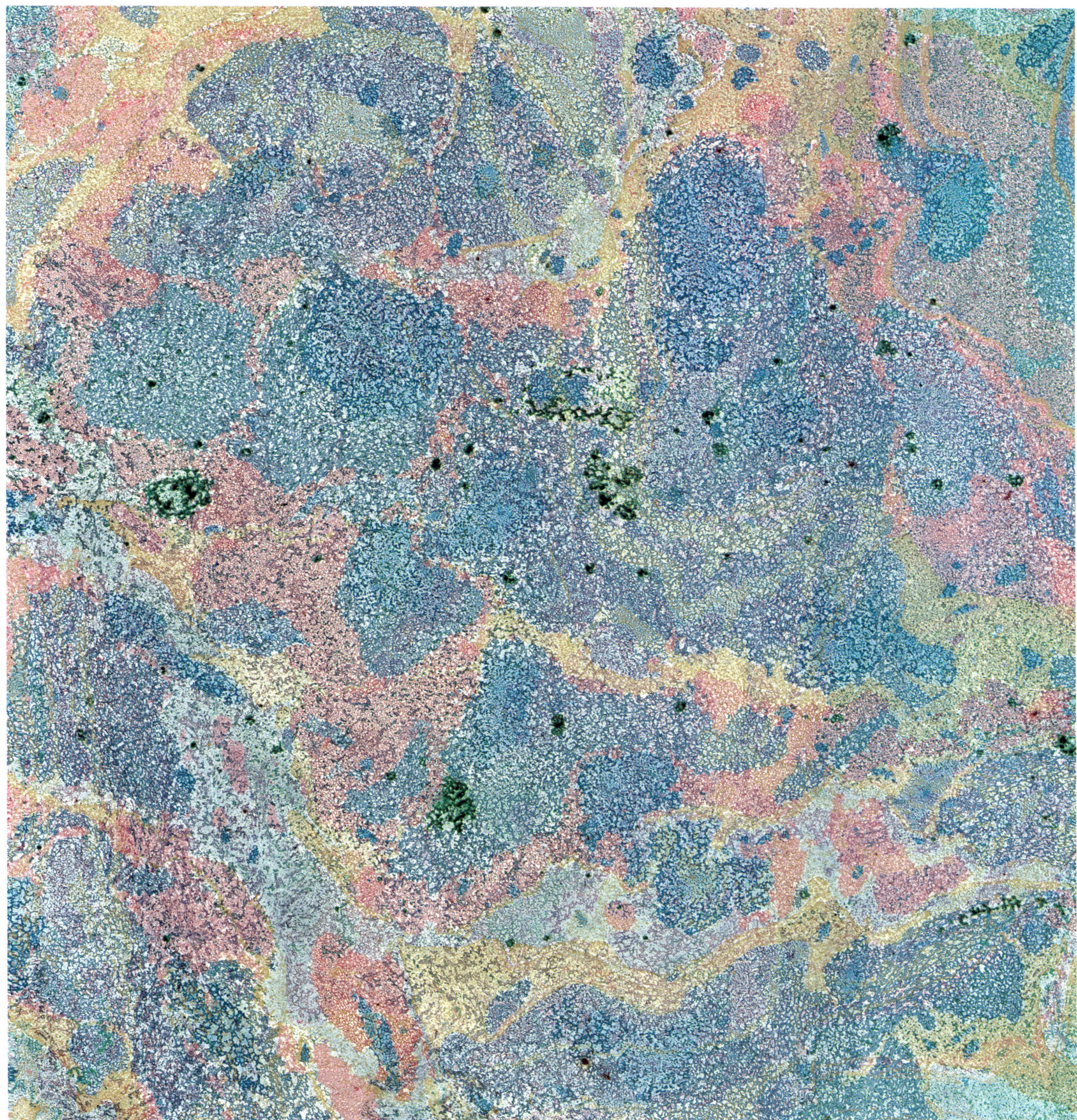

Oil marbling on a carrageenan size by Paul Maurer

Then pour it into your tray, skim off the bubbles, and apply your paints.

Many oil marblers use a carrageenan size because they have experienced the crisp-edged designs it produces for watercolor marbling. However, for oil marbling it makes sense to consider using a methyl cellulose size instead. Methyl cellulose doesn't break down or spoil as rapidly as carrageenan, and it is a bit less expensive. Since the oil-marbled images are feathery anyway, you won't need the pattern definition carrageenan lends.

APPLYING AND PATTERNING THE COLORS

Apply the colors as you would on water (see page 35). Patterning can be done with an assortment of implements, including a stylus, toothpick, hair pick, or piece of broom straw. Rakes and combs can also be made for manipulating colors.

Making a Simple 2-inch (5.1-cm) Rake

To make a simple rake, slip drapery hooks over a piece of ½-inch (1.3-cm) molding at about 2-inch (5.1-cm) intervals. To make a sturdier type of rake that will break up the color into a finer pattern, drill holes into a piece of wood molding and either glue in sharpened dowels or slip in plastic teeth (the kind used for hair curlers). When making either type of rake, be sure to set the teeth far enough apart to allow you to rake in a horizontal as well as a vertical direction.

Making a Simple ¼-inch (0.6-cm) Comb

Balsa wood that is ½ inch (1.3 cm) thick is a good base material for making a simple marbling comb. Cut a strip of wood ¾ to 1 inch (1.9 to 2.5 cm) wide and slightly shorter than the length of your marbling tray. Draw a line lengthwise down the center of the strip. Then, using a yardstick as a guide, mark off ¼-inch (0.6-cm) increments and push T-pins or long, nonrusting dressmaker pins through the wood at each mark. Run a line of waterproof glue over the heads of the pins and glue on a piece of pine to make the comb more sturdy. (Note that because the comb teeth are set closely together, you will only be able to pattern in one direction. To pattern vertically, you'll need to make a second comb slightly shorter than the *width* of your tray.)

Position your marbling tray on a table so that you can reach it whether you're facing it horizontally or vertically. Try patterning and laying the paper from both directions to see which feels most comfortable. Then begin marbling by skimming the size and applying your paints with whisks, brushes, or eyedroppers. You may wish to print the image without patterning, either immediately or after the paints have expanded and reorganized themselves a bit. You can also draw a stylus through your colors to create random designs or follow the diagrams on pages 73–99 to create traditional combed designs. The combed patterns will have soft, rather indistinct edges. Sometimes—especially if you're using Safe Solve as a thinner—they'll also be dappled, with tiny beads of color adding to the design.

Some of the rakes, combs, and a stylus used in oil color marbling. The small free-form comb in the foreground can be made by gluing pins in place and sandwiching them between strips of wood.

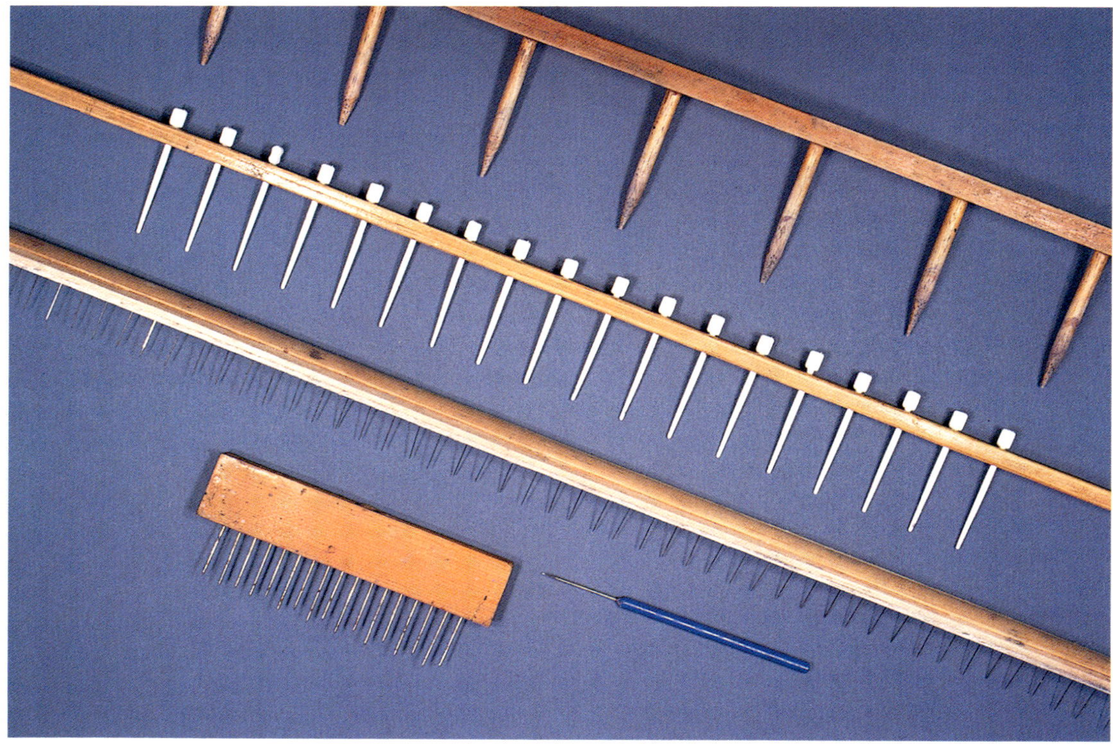

Using a 2-inch (5.1-cm) rake to pattern oil colors on a carrageenan size

Using a 1-inch (2.5-cm) comb to pattern oil colors on a carrageenan size

RINSING AND DRYING

After applying paper to the size and making the print, place your marbled sheet on a rinse board and rinse it with water to remove any excess size. Blot off excess color with paper towels, then carry the sheet to a drying area.

Oil-marbled papers can take a long time to dry—up to several days in very humid conditions. Although drying in damp conditions will keep papers free of wrinkles, you may want to dry your sheets in a warm, sunny area to speed the process. You can later use a warm iron on their unmarbled sides to smooth them.

CLEANUP

Clean brushes, tools, and equipment with solvents (or water, if using Grumbacher MAX oils) to carefully remove all paint residue. Then scrub tools and equipment with a brush and a mild powdered cleanser to remove the solvent film before rinsing thoroughly.

To remove solvent film from brushes, rinse them in warm water and work dish detergent into them. Eyedroppers should be cleaned with solvent and then soap; use a pipe cleaner to reach all parts of the dropper and cap.

Rinse all equipment thoroughly, remembering that any detergent residue will affect color spread in your next marbling session. Reshape the brushes and whisks so they dry in good shape.

To re-create these oil-marbled patterns made on a carrageenan size by Paul Maurer, follow the diagrams and move your rake or comb in the direction of the arrows. Dotted lines indicate previous rake or comb movements.

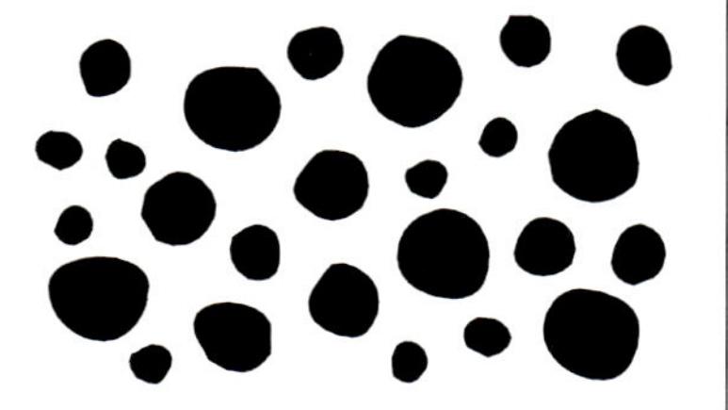

1. Apply color with a whisk or brushes to create a Stone pattern.

2. After applying a Stone pattern, pull a 3-inch (7.6-cm) marbling rake toward you to create the first stage of a Gel Git pattern.

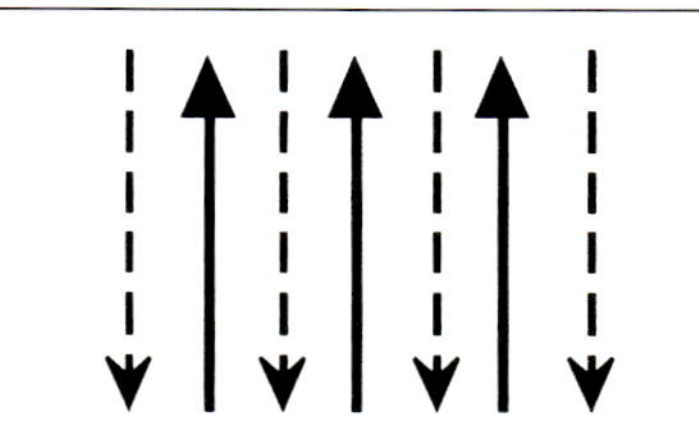

3. After completing step 2, push the rake away from you, bisecting the previous pass to complete the initial vertical Gel Git pattern.

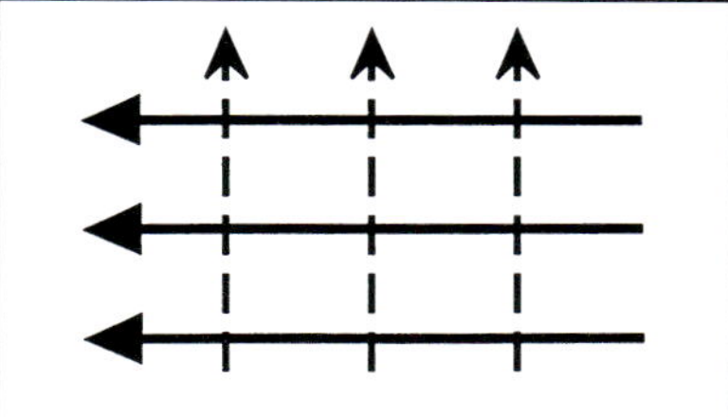

4. Rake right to left across the results of step 3 to begin the horizontal Gel Git pattern.

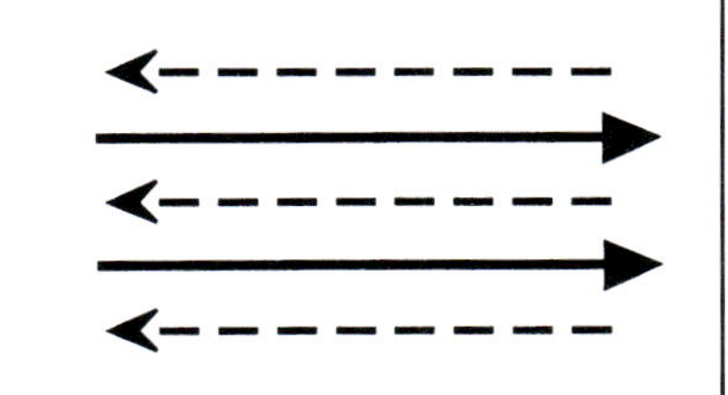

5. Finish the horizontal Gel Git pattern by raking left to right, bisecting the results of step 4.

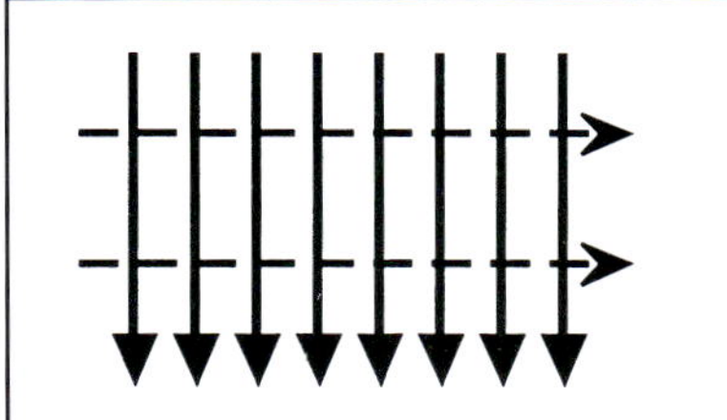

6. Pull a ¼-inch (0.6-cm) comb toward you over the results of step 5 to create a loose Nonpareil design.

Altering the Image with Advanced Techniques

OVERMARBLING

The richness of oil-marbled papers can be heightened by marbling dry sheets a second time. Before overmarbling, make sure papers are as flat as possible so they will print without the air-bubble voids that cockled sheets will produce. Iron the unmarbled sides of any sheets that appear wrinkled. If you have access to a dry-mount press, you can stack papers four or five high and flatten them in only a few seconds.

Double-image oil-marbled papers usually look terrific, no matter what colors you choose. The layering of pigment adds a luminescence to the papers and can also cover small air bubbles that may have been produced in the first marbling. If you are using a thickened marbling size, apply your colors with whisks for a tightly speckled design. Use eyedroppers, pipettes, or brushes for a more open layering of colors.

Apply your paper as carefully as possible, but don't be too disheartened if your first few sheets fight back a bit as you roll them onto the size. The softer absorbent papers used for suminagashi are more easily applied, while the slightly more rigid papers used for other types of marbling can be stiffer and more resistant to rolling. (The more rigid papers are usually less expensive, however, and produce a more vivid image.)

An overmarbled design by Paul Maurer, created on a methyl cellulose size

USING FRISKETS

Floating friskets, as discussed for suminagashi marbling (see page 25), can also be used to mask out areas in oil color marbling, but the results are much better if you use frisket film. Oil colors often run during rinsing and may need blotting to remove paint buildup. They can also remain damp and oily for some time after rinsing. Even a slight oil color sag can ruin a design if the frisket is removed before the color has stopped migrating.

Use frisket film as explained for suminagashi marbling (see page 25), either drawing original images or tracing designs from source material onto the film. Cut the images out with scissors, an X-acto knife, or a swivel knife. Some of the larger punches used in paper crafts might also be used to punch out images from frisket film. A frisket can be created from either the positive images removed from the film or the negative area surrounding the images. Peel the frisket from its paper backing and carefully rub or burnish it onto the sheet to prevent any oil paint from seeping underneath. Then proceed with marbling.

Try applying a frisket to a previously marbled (and flattened) sheet and then overmarbling it to create a more interesting design. Additional friskets can be applied and each paper marbled several times to create complicated and unusual marbled sheets. Sandra Holzman has developed another interesting frisket technique (see below). She applies a tape frisket or resist to her paper before marbling it, and then uses stamping or stencilling techniques to further embellish the dry marbled sheet.

Liquid frisket, also discussed for suminagashi marbling (see page 25), can be used to paint or letter directly on a dry sheet of paper before oil marbling. Apply the liquid frisket and let it dry fully before marbling the sheet. When the oil-marbled paper has *completely* dried, gently peel off the liquid frisket.

An oil-marbled print by Sandra Holzman. Sandra uses tape resists before marbling to preserve unmarbled areas. She then embellishes the dry marbled sheet with stamping and stencilling techniques.

USING COLOR ADDITIVES

There seems to be an unusually large number of would-be alchemists among oil marbling devotees. These adventurous souls, like Paul Maurer and Olaf (no last name), whose work appears here, take special delight in mixing various solvents, oils, and other chemicals with paints and lacquers to see what happens in the marbling tray. The results are sometimes sensational and sometimes ghastly, but always interesting. The thrill of the experience and the constant manipulation of materials, however, makes it difficult to repeat designs or even recall what chemicals were used, not to mention in what quantity or order. As Olaf explains, "After a few sheets, the fickle 'other' in me looks for a way to change even the wonderful, to get a higher version and another jolt of excitement."

Although I cannot provide the exact recipes for the papers pictured here, I can offer some of the materials used by Paul and Olaf. They include:

- Any solvent found in an art supply store or hardware store, such as mineral spirits, turpentine, acetone, kerosene, and naphtha; clove oil and tea tree oil (found in health food stores); alcohol; plate or picture varnishes; bronzing and iridescent powders; old paint flakes; and any other strange ingredients you can think of.
- The above additives are mixed (in tiny amounts at first) into high-quality enamel house paints, sign painter's enamels, artist's oils, printer's inks, silk-screen inks, and lacquers.

Try some oil marbling experiments on your own to make new discoveries and produce novel textures and patterns. Be sure to wear a vapor mask and work outside when experimenting with potentially toxic combinations.

Below, an oil-marbled design created with color additives on a carrageenan size, by Paul Maurer

Right, "As an Absolutist...." by Olaf, 19 x 14 inches (48.3 x 35.6 cm). Artist's oil paints and unknown additives were combined and floated on water to create this image.

MARBLING ON A HOT SIZE

Gabriele Grünebaum, a German marbler, produces exquisite designs that look almost three-dimensional. To create her designs, Gabriele uses a technique she calls "crash marbling," or marbling on a hot size.

The simpler type of crash marbling is done by pouring warm to hot water into your marbling tray, and then dripping artist's tube oil colors diluted with turpentine onto the water. The difference between the temperature of the colors and the warmer temperature of the water causes the colors to swiftly expand and react with each other, creating unusual designs.

For more advanced crash marbling, Gabriele suggests using a metal tray (she recommends zinc). Fill the tray with water or a thin size and place it over a hot plate. When the liquid in the tray is about 100 degrees Fahrenheit (38 degrees Celsius), stir the water to distribute the heat evenly and then wait for the water to stop moving. Apply the paints as explained previously and watch them energetically form bizarre and stunning patterns (see below, left). In her book *Techniques for Marbleizing Paper*, Gabriele cautions that the paper must be applied to the rapidly moving colors quickly to avoid trapping air bubbles. She also notes that this type of oil marbling is best done outdoors, as the heat makes paint and solvent fumes more intense.

MARBLING WITH POLLUTED SIZE

One of Paul's particularly interesting prints was made with thinned printer's inks on a carrageenan size (see below, right). He first let the pattern from the last print remain on the size overnight. The next day, without first skimming off the skin that had formed on the size and color, he applied diluted oil colors. After the paint sat on the size for a few minutes, cracks and bits of floating color appeared.

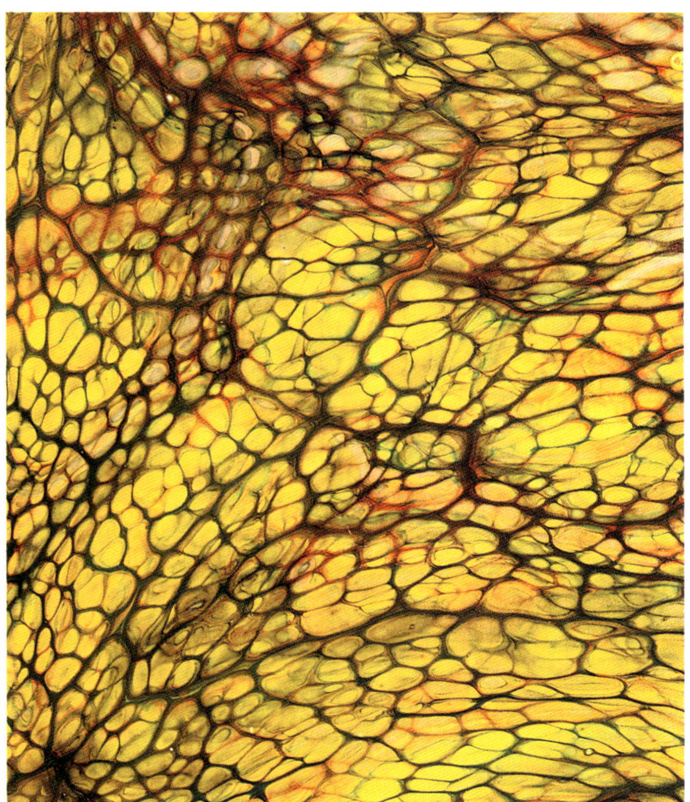

Detail of "Crash Marbling" by Gabriele Grünebaum, 17 x 23¼ inches (43.2 x 59.1 cm). To create her marbled designs, Gabriele uses artist's tube oils, often thinning them as much as 1–1 with turpentine.

Detail of a print by Paul Maurer, made by applying printer's inks to an unskimmed size

APPLYING COLORS IN AN UNUSUAL WAY

Although most marblers use brushes, whisks, or eyedroppers to apply their colors, Hikmet Barutcugil, a Turkish marbler whose stunning work is pictured below, sometimes uses a most unusual method of applying his color. Instead of applying his oil colors directly to the water, Hikmet first puts them on a sheet of glass. He then pours the colors onto the surface of the water. The complicated procedure also involves using mineral dyes and pigment color. Hikmet describes his work: "To create Barut Ebru [the design pictured here] I tried to simulate the process of how real marble is formed in nature. It is a kind of multicolor suminagashi."

"Barut Ebru" by Hikmet Barutcugil, 19⁷⁄₁₀ x 13⁴⁄₅ inches (50 x 35 cm)

SWEDISH MARBLING WITH DILUTED OIL COLORS

Jan-Olov Nyström, a Swedish oil marbler, works with very diluted artist's oil colors that are at least 48 hours old. His delicately spotted images, like the one pictured below, have a subtle, poetic quality about them that is rarely seen in oil color marbling.

Jan-Olov works on a methyl cellulose size with only two or three colors. He thins the colors with mineral spirits until they are so pale "you can hardly see them." To create the design pictured, he first sprinkled very thin black color over the size. Next, he drew a stylus through the black color to make it more even and to draw the color into thin black lines. He then applied blue color (which was at least 48 hours old) in a regular pattern with an eyedropper. The blue color was allowed to expand until it formed square-shaped areas all over the tray. (Jan-Olov cautions that if the color is too thick and does not expand, you will have to remove some of it by dipping small pieces of paper into the color.)

To pattern the blue color, Jan-Olov repeatedly drew a stylus through it, avoiding the black paint, to form a vertical Gel Git. (See page 40 for instructions on creating a vertical Gel Git pattern.) Jan-Olov finished by making a number of horizontal (left to right) passes through the blue paint with the stylus, still avoiding the black paint.

One of Jan-Olov Nyström's poetic images, created with very diluted artist's oil colors

"Sand Dune" by Marie Palowoda, 14¼ x 24 inches (36.2 x 61 cm). Mountainous, free-form designs like this one can be made by applying the paper with erratic movements.

MANIPULATING THE PAPER TO CREATE SHIFTED DESIGNS

MAKING FREE-FORM SHIFTED DESIGNS

If you've perfected the art of smoothly rolling down your paper to make a contact print, it's now time to break the rules and apply the paper with all the grace of a loon coming in for a landing. Use quivering, flopping, and sliding movements as you gradually lay the paper on the marbling size. If you are consistent in your actions and keep your motions tight and repetitive, you can use movement to produce unusual papers with mountainous peaks and valleys. Too much exuberance, however, will produce a wake in your tray and lead to color sinkage. It can also push color away, creating streaks and flashes of paper rather than bands of color.

Work with a small enough sheet of paper and a large enough tray to allow yourself room to maneuver, so that you can experiment with side-to-side and dragging movements. Making your size a little thicker than usual may also be helpful.

You may find this technique a bit frustrating at first, but once you begin seeing how different movements affect the outcome of your designs, you'll start enjoying it and will be on your way to creating papers like the ones pictured.

INSERTING THE PAPER INTO THE MARBLING BATH

Another way to create designs with peaks and valleys is to use a most unconventional method of paper application practiced by Olaf. He inserts his paper vertically into the marbling bath, rocking it from side to side or creating a zig-zag movement with the paper as he lowers it *into* (rather than *onto*) the bath. As Olaf suggests, "Vertical dipping can be done with any hand dance from the glide (smooth, slow, and straight) to the frug (fast and vibrating) to the tango (smooth and angular)," or any combination thereof. Smaller, more rigid papers work best for this type of work, and your marbling tray will have to be rather deep. (A marbling tub would be more appropriate.)

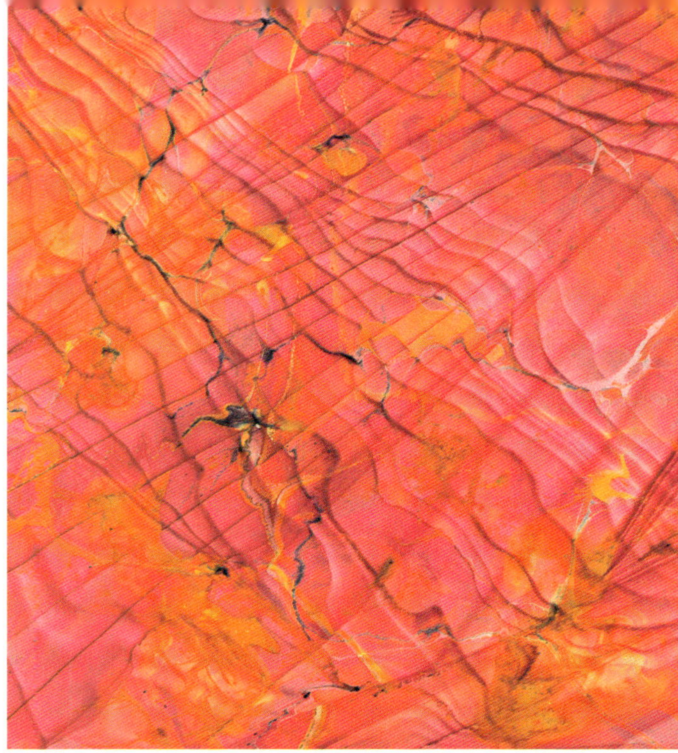

Paul Maurer created this design by using shifting techniques on both layers of a double-image paper.

"Redes" by Olaf, 19 x 12½ inches (48.3 x 31.8 cm). This paper was zig-zagged from side to side as it was lowered into a bucket of water on which the oil colors were floating.

Olaf used artist's oils on water to create this tiny print from his "New Mexico Hills" series, 7 x 3¾ inches (17.8 x 9.5 cm). Olaf often rocks his paper from side to side as he lowers it vertically into (rather than onto) the marbling bath.

MAKING REFINED SHIFTED DESIGNS

Spanish marbling, a technique usually done with watercolor paints and marked by regular diagonal shaded lines (see page 113), can also be attempted with oil colors. This type of shifting is not as freewheeling as those described on page 48. In fact, Spanish marbling requires a great deal of concentration and practice.

Paul Maurer is a master of shifted or "Spanish" marbling, as shown by this oil-marbled paper.

The Spanish marbling technique has a colorful history. According to nineteenth-century marbling lore, it was discovered quite by accident when a marbler reported for work one day still tipsy from the night before. When he began to marble, his hands shook, causing his papers to shake, too; every sheet that he produced contained telltale waved stripes. When the master of the shop saw the "ruined" papers, he wasn't angry but elated, and complimented the marbler on his newly created patterns.

To try this technique, first apply your colors. Then lower the corner of the paper held closest to your body onto the size. Move the hand that holds this corner back and forth in small movements as you very slowly lay the rest of the sheet down. (This can take a full minute or longer.) It's difficult to coordinate the movements of both hands simultaneously to produce a regular pattern with this technique, but the results can be so sensational that most marblers spend a good deal of time experimenting with it. For best results, start with small sheets of paper (9 x 12 inches or 23 x 30.5 cm) and a thicker-than-usual size.

Once you've mastered Spanish marbling, break the rules by deliberately producing a pattern that shows flashes of paper (usually considered a mistake). If it's done with regularity, as in the paper by Paul Maurer shown opposite (top), renegade shifting can be quite beautiful.

Depending upon how the paint is applied before shifting, and how the paper is applied during shifting, shifted patterns can take on very different personalities. For example, the paper can be held by its opposing corners to create the traditional diagonal shading, or it can be laid down in a horizontal format (by holding it in the middle of both long or short ends). The image pictured opposite (bottom) was formed by shifting large and small drops of color in the horizontal format, producing a pattern that looks like pebbles under water.

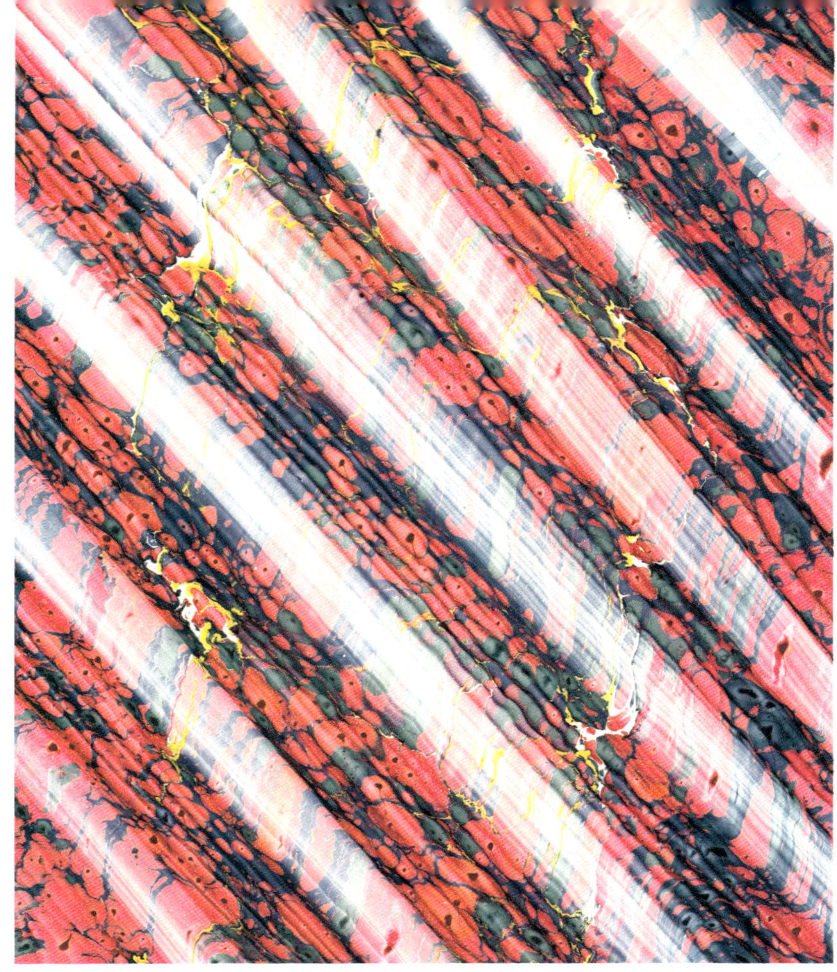

Although flashes of paper are usually seen as a fault, Paul Maurer's design shows how breaking the rules can lead to the creation of a stunning pattern.

A pebble-like shifted design by Paul Maurer

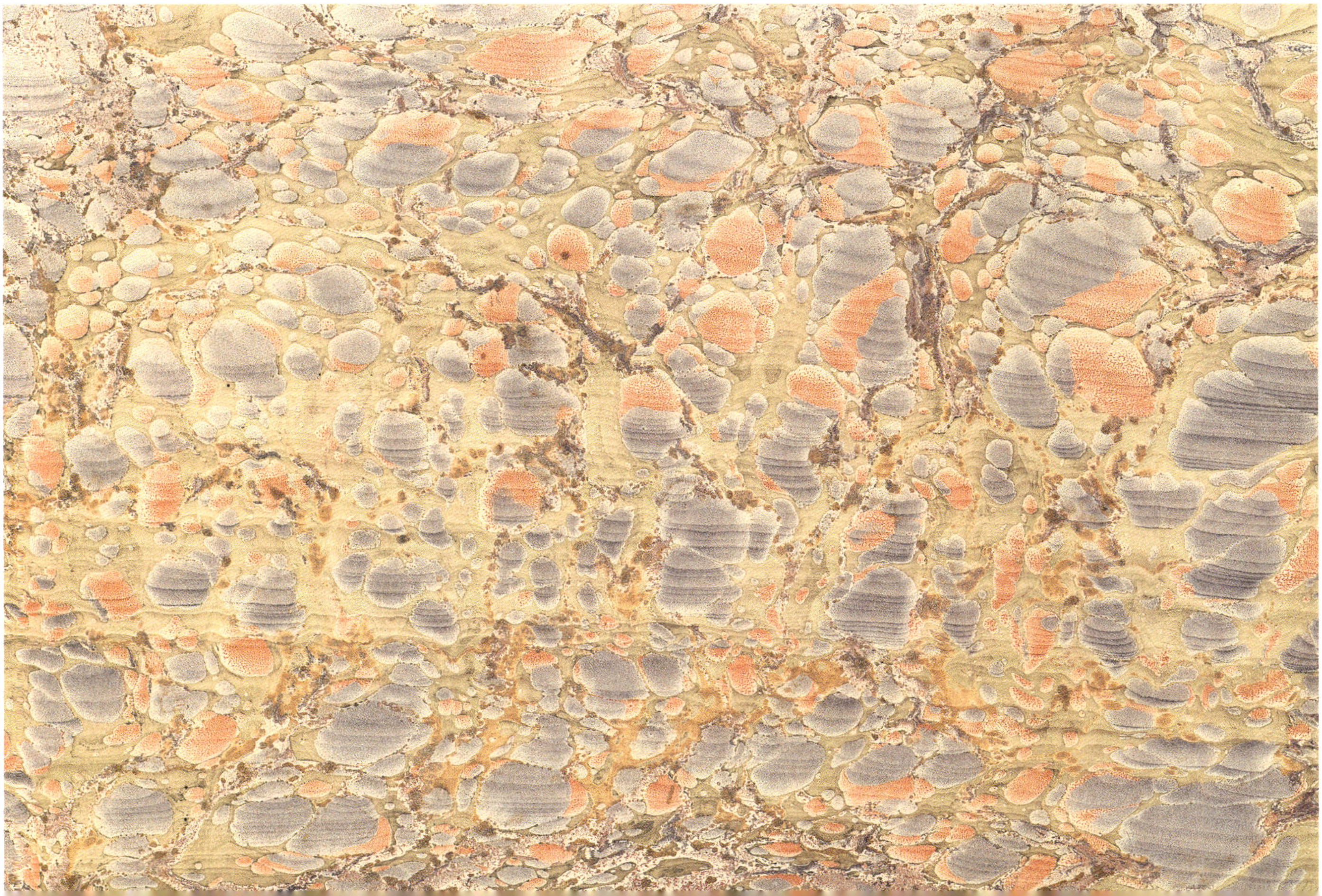

KAY RADCLIFFE'S MALACHITE PATTERNING TECHNIQUES

The photos opposite show Kay Radcliffe, a fine oil marbler and artist, creating the signature malachite designs for which she is well known. Kay was kind enough to share the specifics for making the design, which was done with Winsor & Newton Winsor Green oil paint, black and white oil paints, and black and white oil-base silk-screen inks. She applied these colors to a methyl cellulose size. Kay describes her technique in her own words:

MIXING THE COLORS

"The darkest color used to create this pattern is black, which is formed from a 50-50 mixture of black oil paint and black silk-screen ink. First, put a small amount of mineral spirits in a jar. Add the paints, put the lid on the jar, and cover the lid with a rag. Then shake vigorously. Add more mineral spirits and continue to shake until the mixture is smooth and the consistency of Half and Half—thicker than milk, but thinner than cream.

"Straight Winsor Green is the middle value color, which can be mixed with mineral spirits the same way as the black and to the same consistency. You will notice that this color is intense and the messiest of the paints to work with.

"For the lightest green, use a 50-50 mixure of white oil paint and white silk-screen ink. Then add a small quantity of the mixed Winsor Green. Add the mixed green in a small amount, as it is easier to add more green to white to get the desired color than vice versa."

APPLYING THE COLORS

"It is advisable to experiment with the order in which the colors are applied. I suggest starting with black, then Winsor Green, then light green. Try changing the order of application to see what works best. Using a drop brush to lightly 'throw' the colors onto the size, I suggest trying to apply the colors in rows. If the colors spread too far they will print too lightly; if they remain in small blobs on top of the size they are too thick (although Winsor Green tends not to spread as widely as the other two colors)."

Malachite paper, one of Kay Radcliffe's signature designs

COMBING

"This pattern should not show comb marks, and I've found two ways to create it: with the back of a hair pick, or with a graining comb. Using both in combination works best. Again, you'll need to experiment to find what you prefer. Please note that while the marbled malachite resembles the mineral pattern seen in the real stone, it won't look exactly the same. The aim of re-creating it is to match the color and intensity as closely as possible so that, at a glance, it looks like it *could* be malachite."

(Note: Kay owns the copyright to the malachite design and the techniques described here. She has shared her secrets for your own personal use, but use of this design or techniques for profit would be in violation of her copyright.)

Kay Radcliffe's marbling tray with the drop brushes she used to apply the paints. Notice that she has applied the oil paints in rows.

Kay using a graining comb to pattern oil colors on the methyl cellulose size

Kay applying her paper to the floating oil color. Kay sometimes changes her paper-handling technique to match the personality of the paper she's using.

Kay peeling the marbled paper back from the size. (Photos by Tim Feresten)

USING ADVERSE MARBLING CONDITIONS TO CREATE DESIGNS

If you're marbling outdoors, as Olaf often does, you're subject to the whims of nature. A breeze that suddenly picks up can—if your tray is not fully shielded—yield strange (and wonderful) patterns. "Violet Violence," pictured below, was the result of a sudden breeze and the unusual skimming practices of the marbler. (Olaf uses a hose to add water to his tray and periodically skims by filling the tray to overflow. Although he usually waits for the water to stop moving before applying the paint, he theorizes that water near the bottom of the tray was still moving when he applied his color and captured this print.)

ROLLING THE TRAY TO CREATE WAVE DESIGNS

By placing two large dowels under the marbling tray and rolling the tray vigorously back and forth, you can add interesting, shaded wave effects to oil colors floating on a marbling size. When the size stops moving, make the marbled print.

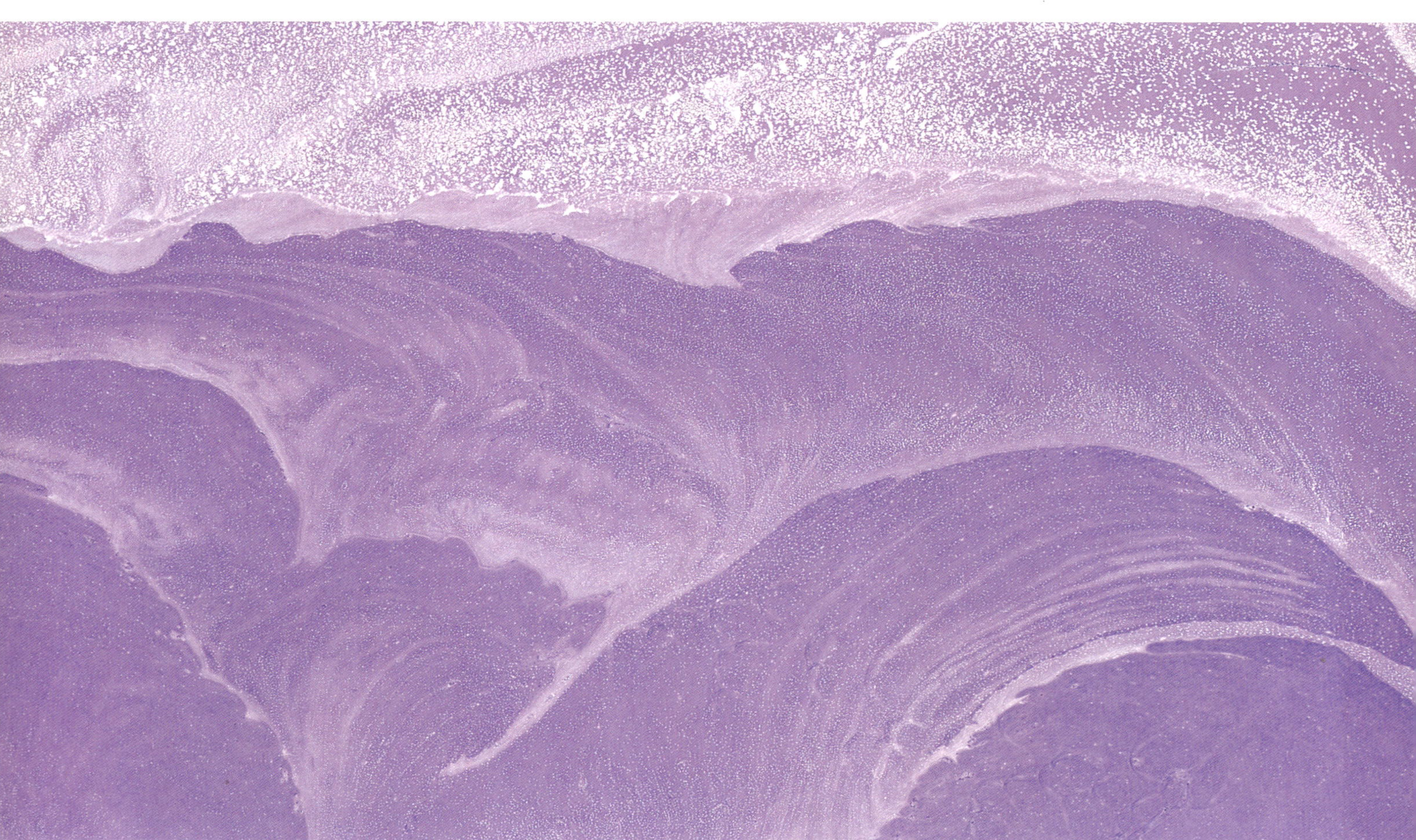

"Violet Violence" by Olaf, 11½ x 20 inches (29.2 x 50.8 cm). A sudden breeze helped create this design.

Troubleshooting

Listed below are some common problems found in oil color marbling, along with their most likely causes and solutions.

Colors sink when applied.

1. Your colors may be too thick. Add more solvent to thin them out a bit.
2. Your colors may not contain enough surfactant; add more to help the colors spread and float.
3. You may be flinging colors down too aggressively. Try using a drop brush and applying color with a back-and-forth wrist movement to soften its impact on the marbling bath. If you're using an eyedropper, choose another method of color delivery that delivers smaller drops of paint.
4. You may not have skimmed your size sufficiently. Be sure to thoroughly skim off any color residue between prints.
5. If the last colors applied are sinking, the surface tension of the size has probably been increased by colors applied previously. Add more surfactant to the colors applied last. You may also try working with fewer colors to decrease surface tension problems.

Colors spread out and then contract and sink.
Your size may be too cold. Stir in a little warm water to heat it.

Color is grainy.

1. Beading or graininess is part of the nature of oil marbling (my favorite part!), especially when working with Safe Solve. Try using another solvent to see if you like the results better.
2. You may be working too slowly. Colors tend to get grainier the longer they sit on the size.

Color is lumpy or gritty.

1. You may not have thoroughly mixed your color. Strain the color and remix it.
2. The color may be old and dried out, or it may be dirty. Try the first suggestion.
3. The chemistry of the color may make it incompatible with the thinning agent.

Color is too pale.
You may have added too much thinner or surfactant to the color. Try adding more stock color to your color mixture or use this color last, when the surface tension created by the preceding colors will impede its spread.

Color streaks during rinsing.
Your color may be too thick or too heavily applied. Blot your paper with the twisted tip of a paper towel or a cotton swab.

You're only using blues and greens, but red shows up in your marbled print.

1. Did you use red on the previous sheet? If the size was not skimmed thoroughly, a red residue may have mixed with your new colors.
2. Blobs of color on the bottom of your tray may be rising to mix with new colors applied.

Unmarbled spots appear on the finished print.

1. For small spots, dust and debris may be floating on the marbling bath when color is applied. Be sure to skim just before applying colors.
2. For large spots, air bubbles trapped under the paper may be creating voids. Take more care applying the paper and letting it roll down onto the size. Keeping your environment humid will also keep paper more supple and cooperative.

Streaks of paper color or more intense color ("shift marks") appear on the marbled print.
You may be sliding or dropping the paper as it's applied. Work more slowly and try to be more consistent in your movements. If problems continue, position your tray so that you face it horizontally when applying the paper. This way, you won't have to reach so far.

3

WATERCOLOR MARBLING

WATERCOLOR MARBLING has been fascinating (and frustrating) artists since the fifteenth century, when the Persians began floating colors on a liquid medium similar to the marbling size used today. Watercolor marbling is both the most complicated and the most rewarding type of marbling, because it allows for so much pattern control. With a little practice and some attention to detail, it can be used to produce either precise combed images or bold fantasy designs.

Unfortunately, the watercolor medium is also a bit temperamental. Variables such as temperature, humidity, and thickness of size and colors must be carefully balanced to achieve optimum results. If you approach watercolor marbling with a willingness to let the medium guide you, however, and don't expect to produce a technically perfect sheet immediately, your efforts will be handsomely rewarded. (The truth is, most people love their first efforts, even with the inevitable dust spots and hesitation marks.)

A collage showing fantasy fish, created by Paul Maurer. Rings of color were deposited on the size before they were teased with a stylus into a fantasy design.

"Sherbet Flame," a traditional watercolor-marbled paper by the author

MATERIALS

To try your hand at what many consider to be magic, you'll need the following equipment:

- *Marbling tray.* If possible, build or buy a divided marbling tray that has a separate skim/rinse section. This will make it easier to rinse papers and will also minimize problems caused by tray pollution. Also, a tray with a white bottom is preferable as it makes floating colors easier to see. To build your own marbling tray with a skim/rinse section, see page 16.
- *Small 8- x 10-inch (20.3- x 25.4-cm) testing tray.* This type of tray allows you to test and adjust your marbling colors without polluting the large marbling tray.
- *Water.* Use distilled water at first to minimize problems, as excess mineral content can influence watercolor marbling. Later, test your tap water to see whether you get the same results.
- *Paper.* Highly absorbent oriental and handmade papers can be used for watercolor marbling, but the image will have a soft, diffused look. Many commercial papers and art papers in various cover, text, and bond weights will produce a crisp marbled image if they are first coated with an alum mordant to help them retain color (see pages 63–64 for instructions on coating paper).

  Papers that work as of this printing are Scott Spectra-Tech (a 70-pound paper is one of my favorites), Canson, Strathmore, Classic Laid, Lana Laid, Classic Linen, and Neenah offset papers. Be sure to add some colored papers to your supplies; they will alter the colors of the paints you apply and increase your color palette.

  Papers to avoid include glossy stock, papers that break down when wet, and papers coated with a calcium buffer that repels alum and color. Although calcium is great for

Some of the materials and equipment used for watercolor marbling

paper longevity, it poses problems for watercolor marblers. Many calcium-coated papers that appear to marble just fine will show color run-off when rinsed, although some marblers have avoided this by marbling the papers within minutes of aluming them, as soon as the surface of the paper is dry. A local printer can help you purchase paper and also check on which papers are coated with calcium.

- *Alum.* Any nonabsorbent paper you use must be coated with a mixture of alum and water to retain color. If you accidentally marble the side of a paper that was not alumed (as every marbler eventually does), you'll see your beautiful image slide off the sheet during rinsing. Alum (aluminum sulfate, aluminum potassium sulfate, or aluminum ammonium sulfate) can be purchased from a marbling or fiber arts supply house.
- *Aluming equipment.* To use the alum, you will need a tablespoon for measuring the dry alum crystals and a 1-quart (1-l) stainless steel or enamel pot (reserved for marbling only) for dissolving the alum. A pint-sized (0.5-l) plastic container with a lid can hold any leftover alum solution. A sponge is also needed for distributing the alum solution. Two sheets of blotter paper and two ½-inch-thick (1.3-cm-thick) boards, all larger than the papers you intend to marble, can sandwich the alumed sheets and keep them flat. Label one of the boards "alum-side up" and the other "alum-side down" to avoid marbling the wrong side of the paper.
- *Carrageenan.* Powdered carrageenan is usually used to make the size for watercolor marbling as it lends excellent image clarity. Various other sizes, like methyl cellulose and gum tragacanth (the original marbling size), are also appropriate for watercolor marbling. Although rarely used by American marblers, gum tragacanth is used by many Turkish marblers because its source—a leguminous plant—is indigenous to Turkey.
- *Equipment for making the size.* You will need a tablespoon, an electric blender, and a large bucket to make the size. A long-handled spoon can be helpful for mixing extra water into the bucket, which may be necessary to maintain the ratio of 2 tablespoons (30 g) of size for every 1 gallon (3.8 l) of water.

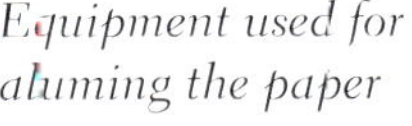
Equipment used for aluming the paper

- *Colors.* Your best bet is to use high-quality water-based marbling colors that are specifically formulated for the craft, available from a marbling supplier. Many watercolors and tube gouaches available in art supply shops can also be used, but they are difficult to get working properly. (For suggestions on working with acrylics, see Chapter 4, pages 124–127.)
- *Ox gall.* This surfactant, like Photo-Flo, helps colors float and spread on the water. It is available through marbling suppliers. Photo-Flo can also be used, but is not preferred for watercolor marbling because it can become sudsy. (Note: If working with acrylic colors, you *must* use Photo-Flo.)
- *Color applicators.* Whisks, eyedroppers, and bamboo brushes—like those described on page 18—can be used. Plastic dropper bottles with a ceramic pie weight or marble inside to stir the color can also be used. Novices should start out by using whisks, which deliver smaller droplets of color that are more likely to float.

  When making a whisk (see page 33), be sure to either invest in broom straw from a marbling supplier or buy a new corn broom. A frustrated marbler called me one day insisting that the colors I'd sold her were no good because they sank no matter what she did. After much detective work, I discovered that she'd made her whisks from an old broom originally used as a cleaning tool and coated with all sorts of unknown chemicals. Such broom straw may have worked fine for oil color marbling, but watercolor puts up with no such indiscretions.
- *Color containers.* Glass jars, plastic jars, or yogurt containers that are big enough to hold a whisk will work fine. I like to use canning jars as they can be boiled and sterilized for reuse in case the color gets moldy. Be sure that any container you use has a tight-fitting lid.
- *Patterning tools.* Purchase or make a rake and combs with various tooth spacings. (Less space between the teeth results in finer patterns.) Try to make or buy combs with teeth spaced from ⅛ to 1 inch (0.3 to 2.5 cm) for lots of patterning options. Some marblers make combs with ultra-thin botanical pins spaced only 1⁄16 inch (0.16 cm) apart to create incredibly fine patterns. A stylus or weaving needle can also be used to pattern colors and tease them into designs.

  A rake has teeth spaced 2 inches (5.1 cm) or more apart, allowing you to use it in either a horizontal or vertical direction. Comb teeth, however, are set closely together, so you will need short combs to pattern vertically, and longer combs to use in a horizontal direction. Instructions for making a simple ¼-inch (0.6-cm) comb and 2-inch (5.1-cm) rake appear in the chapter on oil color marbling (see page 38). Instructions for making a ¼-inch (0.6-cm) Nonpareil comb and a 1-inch (2.5-cm) Bouquet comb—both indispensable tools for watercolor marbling—are provided on the opposite page.
- *Rinsing equipment.* You will need a container for holding rinse water, a bucket, and a paper support like that used for oil marbling (see page 33).
- *Newspaper skim strips and waste receptacle.*
- *Skim board.* A narrow skim board, cut slightly shorter than the width of your tray, is used to remove bubbles from the marbling size. A thin strip of balsa wood about 2 inches (5.1 cm) wide is ideal, although a piece of a wooden yardstick can also be used.
- *Thin surgical gloves or barrier hand cream.* Even watercolor paints can contain materials that may be harmful for your skin. It's safest to protect yourself by using hand protection.
- *Humidifier and air cleaner (optional).* While these supplies are optional, they are necessary if you intend to produce high-quality dust-free sheets.
- *Drying racks or clothesline strung with PVC pipe.* See page 18 for more information.
- *Cleanup equipment.* A new scrub brush or sponge should be used for cleaning tools and trays. Never use soap as soap residue can cause major marbling problems.

Additional equipment used for advanced techniques will be noted in that section.

MAKING A ¼" (0.6-CM) NONPAREIL COMB

1. Cut two strips of pine, each ¼ inch (0.6 cm) thick, 1 inch (2.5 cm) wide, and slightly shorter than the width of your marbling tray. (Note: You will also need to make a second Nonpareil comb, with strips slightly shorter than the *length* of your tray. The two combs will allow you to pattern in either direction.)
2. Sand both strips of wood. Draw a line down the center of one strip and use a yardstick to mark off ¼-inch (0.6-cm) increments.
3. Apply a line of waterproof glue to the marked-off strip.
4. Set long, nonrusting dressmaker pins in the glue, staggering heads as necessary.
5. Apply a second line of glue over the pinheads and allow it to dry.
6. Glue the second strip of wood on top of the pinheads and clamp to dry.

Although they will not be as sturdy, Nonpareil combs can also be made by tapping the points of pins into a strip of pine with a hammer.

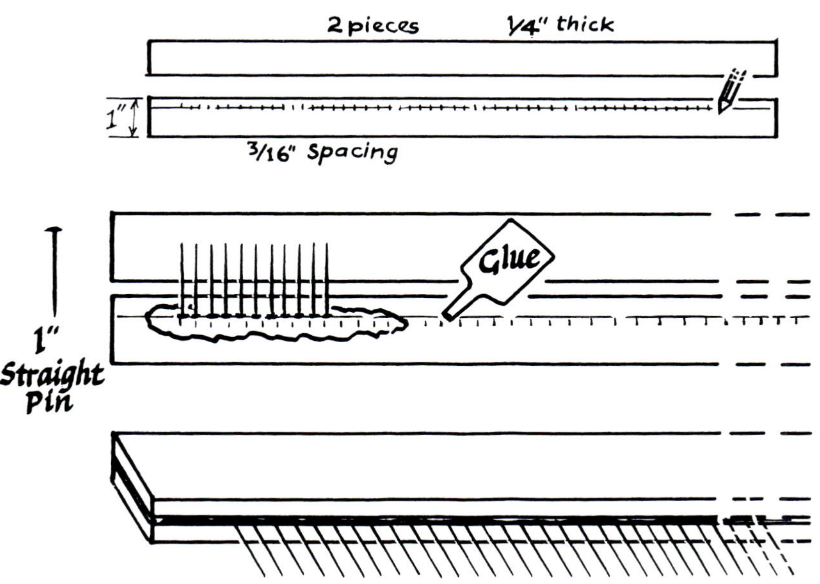

MAKING A 1" (2.5-CM) BOUQUET COMB

1. Cut a strip of pine ¼ inch (0.6 cm) thick, 1½ inches (3.8 cm) wide, and slightly shorter than the width of your marbling tray. (See note in step 1 for Nonpareil combs, above.)
2. Mark off and drill two staggered rows of 1⁄16-inch (0.16-cm) holes 1 inch (2.5 cm) apart along the length of the pine strip.
3. Insert T-pins or haircurler rods into the holes. Stabilize each pin or rod with a spot of waterproof glue where it pierces the comb base.
4. Glue the second strip of wood on top of the pinheads and clamp to dry.

Another type of Bouquet comb can be made by drilling holes into Plexiglas and inserting haircurler rods into the openings. The added advantage of this type of comb is that you can see through it while creating the sometimes tricky Bouquet pattern.

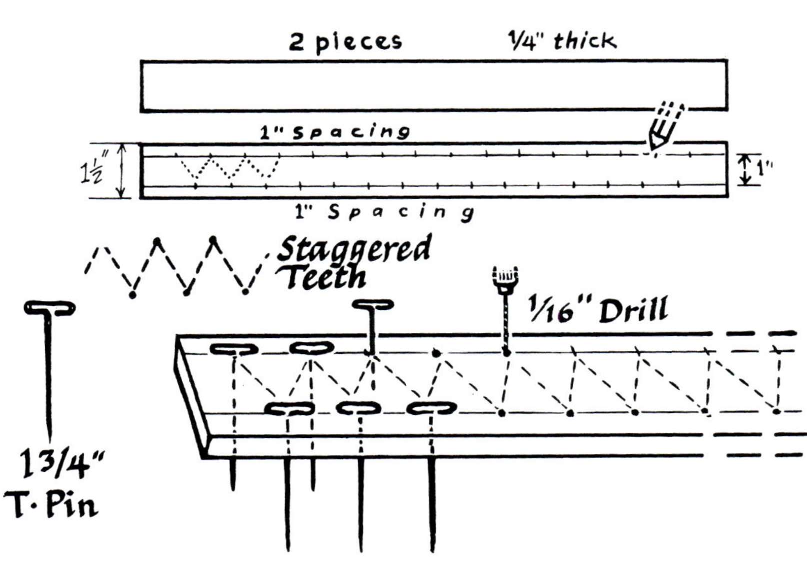

THE WORKSPACE

Although watercolor marbling can be practiced in almost any environment, a cool (50- to 65-degree Fahrenheit or 10- to 18-degree Celsius), humid, and dust-free environment will keep problems to a minimum. Dust can be a serious problem if you're trying to produce fine combed designs, as the smallest particle can cause a void or unpatterned spot on marbled papers. When working on papers for reproduction, which must be as free of defects as possible, I not only keep my pets out of the marbling studio, but change my clothes before coming upstairs to avoid bringing their fur and dander back to the marbling tray. (Stray whiskers, however, are welcomed as patterning tools.)

Humidity is important as it keeps the papers supple and more cooperative as you lay them on the floating colors. Humidity also keeps dust down and helps prevent a skin from forming on the size. It is a good idea to use a humidifier and keep a spray bottle nearby to mist the air occasionally. Avoid air conditioning as it tends to dry out the air. If you are working in very hot temperatures, mix a thicker size to maintain pattern control.

You should also avoid drafts and direct sunlight. They can dry out the colors and cause variations in the surface tension of the size that can lead to color sinkage and malformed patterns. Sunlight can also heat up the colors or size enough to cause problems; if the colors and size aren't within a few degrees temperature of each other, the colors will sink. A panicking marbler with a class full of annoyed high school students called one day to find out why her colors were suddenly sinking. We tracked the problem to her habit of placing colors on a nearby radiator. This was harmless during the summer, but not when the heat was on!

Although there are many ways to set up a marbling studio,the table you use for your tray should be high enough so that you can pattern colors without bending over. A couple of wooden blocks set under the table's legs can make a big difference in how your back feels at the end of a session. Also, use a table that is big enough to hold tools and colors along with the marbling tray. Finally, the tray should be positioned on the table so as to allow you to easily face the tray while patterning colors in either a horizontal or vertical direction.

Galen Berry applied color in diagonal stripes and then executed a Bouquet pattern to create this image.

Basic Techniques

MAKING THE SIZE

Follow the directions on page 36 for making a carrageenan blender size. Be sure to tap the carrageenan into the blender slowly so you don't wind up with clumps and knots of jelly in your size. The mixture should be well homogenized and about the consistency of milk. When you've completed the ratio of 2 level tablespoons (30 g) of carrageenan to 1 gallon (3.8 l) of water, pour the mixture into your marbling tray to a depth of abut 1½ inches (3.8 cm) and cover it to keep out dust.

As you gain experience in watercolor marbling, you can learn to alter the depth and consistency of the size to achieve various purposes and effects. A thinner size tends to allow patterns to wander more, but also gives you the best pattern definition, with thin sharp lines and curves. A slightly thicker or shallower size decreases pattern movement and makes it easier to create a Chevron or Bouquet design (discussed on pages 93 and 90). However you make the size, it's best to wait about 12 hours for it to mature, as watercolor images look quite fuzzy on freshly-made size.

The length of time the size will last depends upon the temperature of your studio or workspace and the amount of watercolor marbling you've done. You can usually produce crisp patterns for about three days. After that, images start to look muddy, the size gets thin and fishy-smelling, and the colors start to sink. Although older size can't be used for fine combing, it can still be used for experimental designs.

Some marblers like to use a size preservative, like borax or formaldehyde, to get a few more days out of their size. Others prolong the size's breakdown by adding fresh extra-thick size to their tray each day, thus managing to use their size for several weeks.

SKIMMING

Most of the air bubbles introduced by blending will dissipate as the size matures. Use the skim board to remove any bubbles that remain before you begin to marble. Newspaper skim strips should be used as described in previous chapters to remove dust and excess color between prints (see page 19). Be very careful not to let color escape around the strip as you drag it down the length of the tray. If you're working in a tray with a skim/rinse section, you'll be able to bring the strip up and over the edge of the divider to avoid color backwash that can pollute your size and accelerate its spoilage.

I often place the skim strip against the wet skim board and use both in tandem when skimming. This trick, learned when I broke my arm and had to marble one-handed for a while, reduces the need for repeated passes with a skim strip.

Another way to reduce tray pollution and make skimming easier is to make sure that your paper fits the tray with only 1 inch (2.5 cm) or so surrounding it. If you apply a large quantity of color to a big tray and then marble a small sheet of paper, you'll have an awful lot of excess color to skim off! One way around this problem is to lay newspaper strips around the perimeter of the tray before applying the color, thereby reducing the size of the tray. (Unfortunately, this technique cannot be used when making combed or raked patterns as the newspaper strips will interfere with use of the comb or rake.)

Some marblers without skim sections in their trays lay sheets of newspaper on the excess color to remove it. Although this works, the newspapers will soak up size along with the excess color, rapidly depleting the amount you have to work with. You can also pick up excess color by marbling envelopes.

ALUMING THE PAPER

Before a sheet of paper can be marbled with water-based paints, it must be treated with an alum solution to make the sheet receptive to the colors. To prepare the alum solution, place 2 tablespoons (30 g) of alum cystals in a pot reserved for this purpose. Add 1 pint (0.5 l) of very hot water (unless you're using the type of alum that dissolves in room-temperature water) and stir to dissolve the alum. You can also heat the mixture on a stove to dissolve the crystals.

When the solution has cooled, protect your hands with rubber gloves and place a sponge in the alum solution. Wring out the sponge so it's not dripping wet and wipe the solution onto the paper. (I like to work over a sheet of Plexiglas, but aluming can be done on any surface that won't be harmed by the solution.) Sponge the alum solution on with overlapping strokes, being sure to moisten (but not soak) every part of the paper. Missed areas will show up as uncolored streaks, while overly saturated sheets will take a long time to dry and will probably wrinkle in the process.

To create a stack of about a dozen alumed sheets, first lay a sheet of blotter paper on top of the inverted aluming board marked "alum-side down." After you alum your first sheet, lay it on top of the blotter paper, alum-side up. As you continue aluming sheets, stack them on top of each other (still alum-side up). Cover the last sheet with another piece of blotter paper and cover the blotter with the second aluming board, marked "alum-side up." Then invert the entire alum stack.

The paper will now be alum-side down, with the sheets moistened first lying on top of the stack. If the sheets are dry to the touch, without visible moisture, they're ready to be marbled. The boards should keep the papers flat, and the blotters will help to keep the papers from drying out so rapidly that they cockle when you try to lay them on the floating colors. If you're working in dry conditions and have difficulty flattening the alumed sheets, try adding another sheet of blotter paper after aluming six sheets. You can also let the papers rest under the aluming boards overnight to help flatten them.

CREATING A MARBLING PALETTE

Although suminagashi- and oil-marbled papers usually contain only a few colors, watercolor-marbled designs may contain many different hues. Your personal color preference will no doubt lead you to choose certain colors for your marbling palette. Many marblers are known for their emphasis on subtle pastel colors, others for their bold primary color schemes.

If you find that your patterns are too busy, have colors that don't harmonize, or are dull and boring, there are several ways to remedy the situation. First, look at colors in nature (my flower garden always inspires me), other pieces of art, fabric, or wrapping papers that show effective color combinations. Take photos and collect swatches of fabrics and papers to create a notebook of reference images.

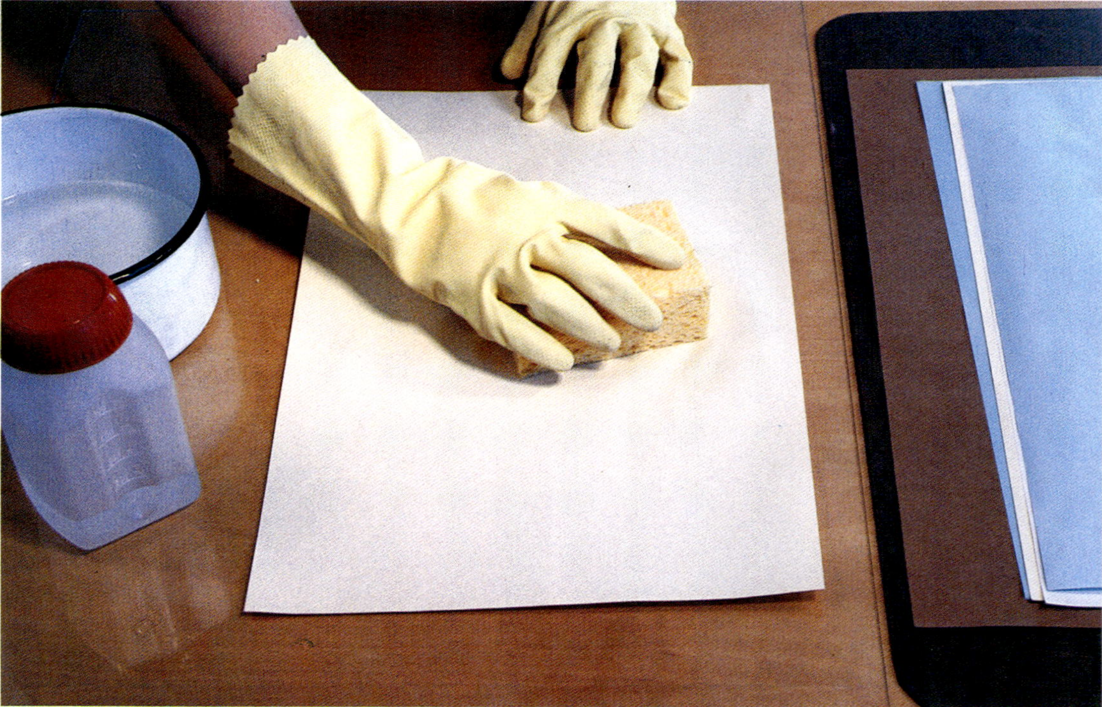

Apply the alum and water carefully in overlapping strokes to avoid missing any areas.

Over twenty colors were applied to create "Rainbow Balloon," by Galen Berry. Image size is 25 x 19 inches (63.5 x 48.3 cm).

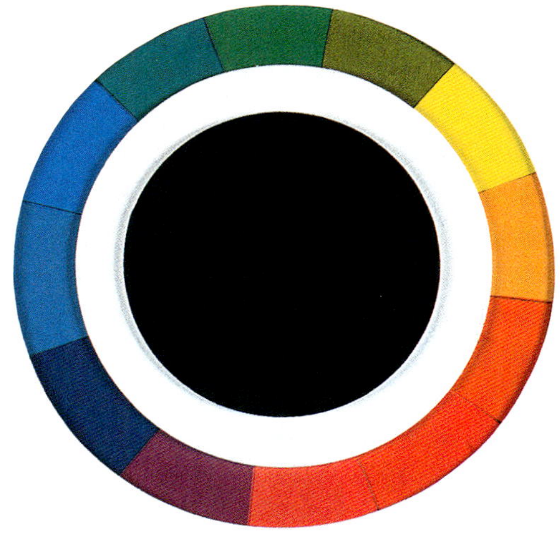

A color wheel showing the primary, secondary, and tertiary colors. An infinite number of hues can be created by mixing the three primary colors (red, blue, and yellow).

Next, buy yourself a color-mixing guide. This can help you mix the three *primary colors*—red, blue, and yellow—to produce a wide range of hues. In addition to the three primary colors, the color wheel above shows the three *secondary colors*—purple, orange, and green—which are created by mixing two primary colors (for example, yellow + blue = green), and the six *tertiary colors*—blue-violet, blue-green, yellow-green, and so on—which are created by mixing a primary color with an adjacent secondary color (for example, yellow + green = yellow-green). The guide will show you how to mix paints in various proportions to create the colors you desire. It can also help you increase your palette by changing a color's value—making it lighter or darker—either by *tinting* the color with white paint or *shading* it with black.

Many successful marbled designs are *monochromatic*, or based on one color, with lighter and darker shades of that color adding interest to the work. Another harmonious color scheme is made up of *analogous* colors—three different colors in close proximity on the color wheel. Some of my favorite designs are based on the hues green, blue-green, and purple. Each of these colors contains a common ingredient: blue. The colors may be tinted or shaded to create a variety of values and intensities.

Most designs can also be energized by introducing a color that provides contrast. For example, if you're working in cool colors—greens, blues, and violets—adding a bit of a hot color like orange, red, or yellow can give your design more impact.

MIXING THE COLOR

If your marbling colors come with instructions, follow them. Otherwise, thoroughly stir the stock color to get any settled pigment back into suspension. Some of this settled color can be very dense. If that is the case, pour most of the liquid out into a clean container and then stir the remaining settled color. Pour the reserved color back into the jar, stir, and continue.

Use distilled water to dilute the color to the consistency of milk. Always start with a small amount of stock color—about 2 tablespoons (30 ml)—to avoid ruining a whole batch if you make a mistake. (Also, although stock color has an indefinite shelf life, its shelf life is limited once it has been mixed with ox gall.) If you're using concentrated marbling paint, you can often add twice as much water and still maintain opacity. When diluting marbling ink, add less water to maintain color intensity.

MIXING TUBE GOUACHE

I don't recommend tube gouache to beginners, but once you've gained experience marbling you may want to experiment with Winsor & Newton Designers' Gouache. To mix it, squeeze out about 2 tablespoons (30 ml) into your color container. Add distilled water sparingly to bring the gouache from a paste to a cream. Then add enough distilled water to bring it to a medium cream consistency. But be forewarned: some colors work, others don't, and the chemical makeup of colors can change from batch to batch of the same color. Colors that usually work are Cadmium Red, Yellow Ochre, Indigo, Lamp Black, and Permanent White.

MAKING METALLIC COLORS

Mica particles, sold by papermaking supply houses, can be mixed into diluted marbling color to make metallic paints. I usually add about 1 teaspoon (4.7 g) of mica to ⅓ cup (80 ml) of color. The trick to working with mica is to stir it into the color well before applying it. (Note: A mask should be worn when working with mica particles to avoid inhaling them.)

ADDING OX GALL TO COLORS AND TESTING COLORS

Ox gall (the bile of an ox) is added to diluted color for several reasons. Ox gall helps water-based colors overcome the surface tension of the size so they can float and spread. Also, it reacts with the alum to help bond the colors to the paper. Finally, ox gall forms a microscopic wall of fat around each color particle that keeps colors from blending together when they're manipulated.

Usually, if you're working with a strong ox gall solution (brown in color), a single drop will adjust ⅓ cup (80 ml) of diluted color. If the ox gall and color are stirred thoroughly, the color should float just fine. If you're using a weak ox gall solution, you may need two drops, but rarely more than that.

Start by adding one drop of ox gall to each of your diluted colors. Stir, then use an eyedropper to apply the colors to your skimmed testing tray. Each color should float and spread into a 1- to 4-inch (2.5- to 10.2-cm) circle without contracting and sinking. Test all the colors individually and then test them together, adding a second drop of ox gall to any colors that are reluctant to stay afloat.

It may be difficult for novices to totally eliminate color sinkage. To maximize your chances, make sure you always skim the size, stir your colors before applying them, and apply colors with a whisk.

APPLYING THE COLORS

Your marbling patterns will vary according to the type of tool used to apply color, the amount of color applied, and the way color is distributed. In general, the first color applied will be the darkest as it is "squeezed" by the colors that follow. Many marblers trying to create a dark black will use that color first. (If black is added last, it may become grey.) The last color applied will usually predominate in a design.

To apply colors with a dropper bottle, hold the bottle close to the surface of the size and squeeze it gently to release (rather than squirt) a drop of color.

Marie Palowoda using dropper bottles to create a particularly graphic image on the marbling size

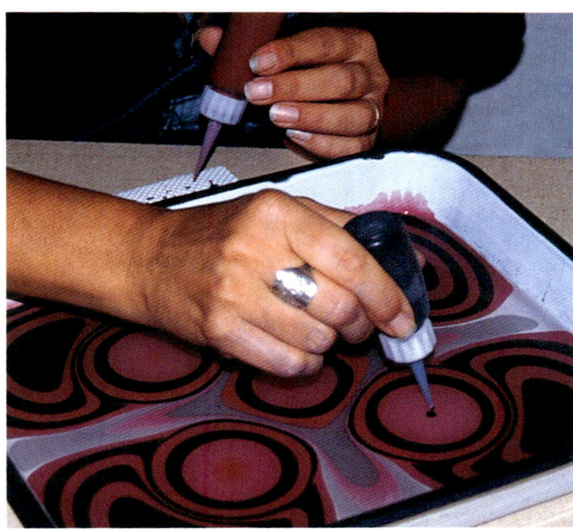

"Sumi Study," Marie's finished print, on the rinse board

To apply colors with an eyedropper, use it as described for oil color marbling, being careful to hold the dropper close to the surface of the size (see page 35). Also, remember to maintain pressure on the dropper bulb so as not to draw air into the dropper. A dropper bottle is used in much the same way. First, shake the bottle from side to side to activate the stirring bead. Then hold the bottle close to the size and squeeze it gently to drop, rather than squirt, the color.

To apply colors that will produce the most regular and vivid combed patterns, use a dropper bottle or eyedropper to apply rings of color in a regular pattern throughout the tray. The rings of color can also be left uncombed to create a striking graphic design, like that created by Marie Palowoda (shown at left). Be aware, however, that because it takes more time to apply color this way, the risk of dust contamination is greater.

The whisk is the tool of choice for novices and anyone wanting to make a good Stone pattern. Use it as described for oil color marbling (see page 34), stirring and tapping off excess color before tapping the whisk against your finger or a dowel. Apply one color over another until the surface of the size is sprinkled with paint. If you want a more intense color, do several whisk applications of the same color. You can also create color blends by using an eyedropper to deposit several different colors in the same whisk.

Colors may also be applied with bamboo brushes. To use a bamboo brush correctly, snap your wrist to release color from the brush. Be careful not to apply the colors too vigorously or they may sink.

No matter what tool you use to deliver the color, remember to stir the color thoroughly each time you apply it. When marbling with watercolors, it's also important to work as quickly as possible to minimize dust contamination.

USING GALL WATER

A dispersant solution called gall water, or "invisible color," is made by adding one drop of ox gall to ⅓ cup (80 ml) of distilled water. Gall water can be applied to floating colors to create clear areas for design use. It can also be used to compress floating colors and intensify their pigmentation. I often use gall water after applying six or seven colors to sharpen the colors and create clear areas where the color of the paper will show through.

PATTERNING THE COLORS

Colors applied with a whisk, eyedropper, dropper bottle, or brush can be printed without patterning, or you can use a stylus to create random designs. You can also create fantasy flower, plant, and animal designs by manipulating rings of color deposited with a brush, eyedropper, or dropper bottle. The illustrations on pages 70–99 show you how to execute some fantasy designs and many traditional raked and combed patterns. Once you understand how patterns and shapes evolve from comb, rake, and stylus movements, you'll be able to simulate specific designs and copy historic patterns yourself.

MAKING THE PRINT

To apply your alumed paper onto the patterned colors, first lift the alum stack cover, pull out a sheet of paper, and replace the cover. Hold the sheet alum-side down by diagonal corners, letting it droop slightly in the middle as you carry it to the marbling tray. Steady one hand on the far corner of the tray and, without letting go of the paper, ease the far edge of the sheet onto the color. Let the rest of the sheet roll down in one smooth motion; don't let go until the sheet has made complete contact with the marbled design.

Because any interruption in a patterned paper will be noticeable, it's especially important to lay the sheet down without shifting or flopping it. These movements can create hesitation or shift marks, or trap an air bubble beneath the paper. After the print is made (immediately upon contact with the floating colors), it won't be disturbed by movement and can be safely pulled back onto the rinse board.

RINSING AND DRYING

Place your rinse board in the drain section of the tray and position the rinse bucket below it. (If you're not using a professional tray, hold your rinse board over a bucket or sink.) Wet the rinse board to keep the first sheet from sliding off, and place your wet marbled print on it. (Avoid touching the wet print as it may smear.) Pour tap water over the print to remove any excess color or size still clinging to the sheet. Then carry the wet sheet to the drying area and drape it over a rack or lengths of PVC pipe strung on a clothesline.

CLEANUP

Use plain water and a scrub brush to clean your equipment. Hold brushes, whisks, and combs under running water to clean them.

Never use any soaps or detergents on your watercolor marbling equipment; any residue of soaps of other chemicals will make color sink or react in unpredictable ways.

MARBLING ENVELOPES

Envelopes must be handled slightly differently than flat papers. Like flat papers, they must be alumed, but it's best to keep them out of the alum stack where their gummed flaps may stick to other papers. They may also make a crimp in papers stacked above and beneath them. Instead, set the alumed envelopes aside with their flaps open to be marbled when dry.

To marble an envelope, hold it parallel to the size surface and slowly tip it onto the marbled pattern. Rinse and dry it with the flap open. To make envelopes light enough to address without using a label, use the residue of color from a previous print or create pastel colors that you can letter over with standard ink. You can also use gall water to create a clear area in the pattern for addressing, or letter over dark patterns with white or metallic ink.

A flower fantasy design by Turkish marbler Beki Almaleh, $9\frac{1}{2}$ x $6\frac{3}{10}$ inches (24 x 16 cm). The traditional method of creating these marbled paintings is to first create a marbled design (usually a Stone pattern) and then begin the fantasy image.

A Guide to Creating Classical Watercolor-Marbled Designs

FANTASY DESIGNS

Fantasy designs are based on the plant and animal motifs seen in Persian marbling. As these designs take time to execute, they're often done over a Stone pattern (see page 72), in which the inevitable dust spots won't be as noticeable.

To create fantasy designs, first apply color with an eyedropper. Then use a stylus to push and pull the expanded dots of color into abstract flowers, birds, fish, butterflies, and hearts, as shown below and opposite. (The solid arrows in the illustrations show where to penetrate the circle of color and whether to draw the stylus partially or completely through it. The dotted lines indicate previous stylus movements.)

Three plant and flower designs

Fantasy fish

Fantasy bird

An abstract design

A heart, a butterfly

TRADITIONAL MARBLED PATTERNS

Many marbled patterns are based on specific ways of applying or combing color. The range of images you can create is extended by the fact that patterns will look different depending on what size comb or rake you use to create them. To create the patterns pictured in this section, use the tool size noted. You should also feel free, however, to experiment with other equipment sizes.

As you practice these designs, you will find that most are based on four basic patterns: Stone, Gel Git, Nonpareil, and Chevron. You'll also learn that new patterns are easily made by modifying others.

To create each pattern, follow the steps shown next to the design. Move your comb, rake, or stylus in the direction of the arrows. Dotted lines indicate previous comb or rake movements.

PATTERNS BASED ON STONE OR ROCK DESIGNS

Basic Stone or Rock

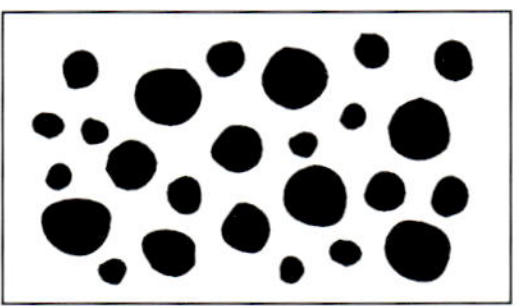

Apply colors with a whisk for a tiny Stone design or with a brush for a design representing larger rocks and pebbles. Begin in the center of the tray and move your arms in a circular direction as you broadcast color throughout the tray.

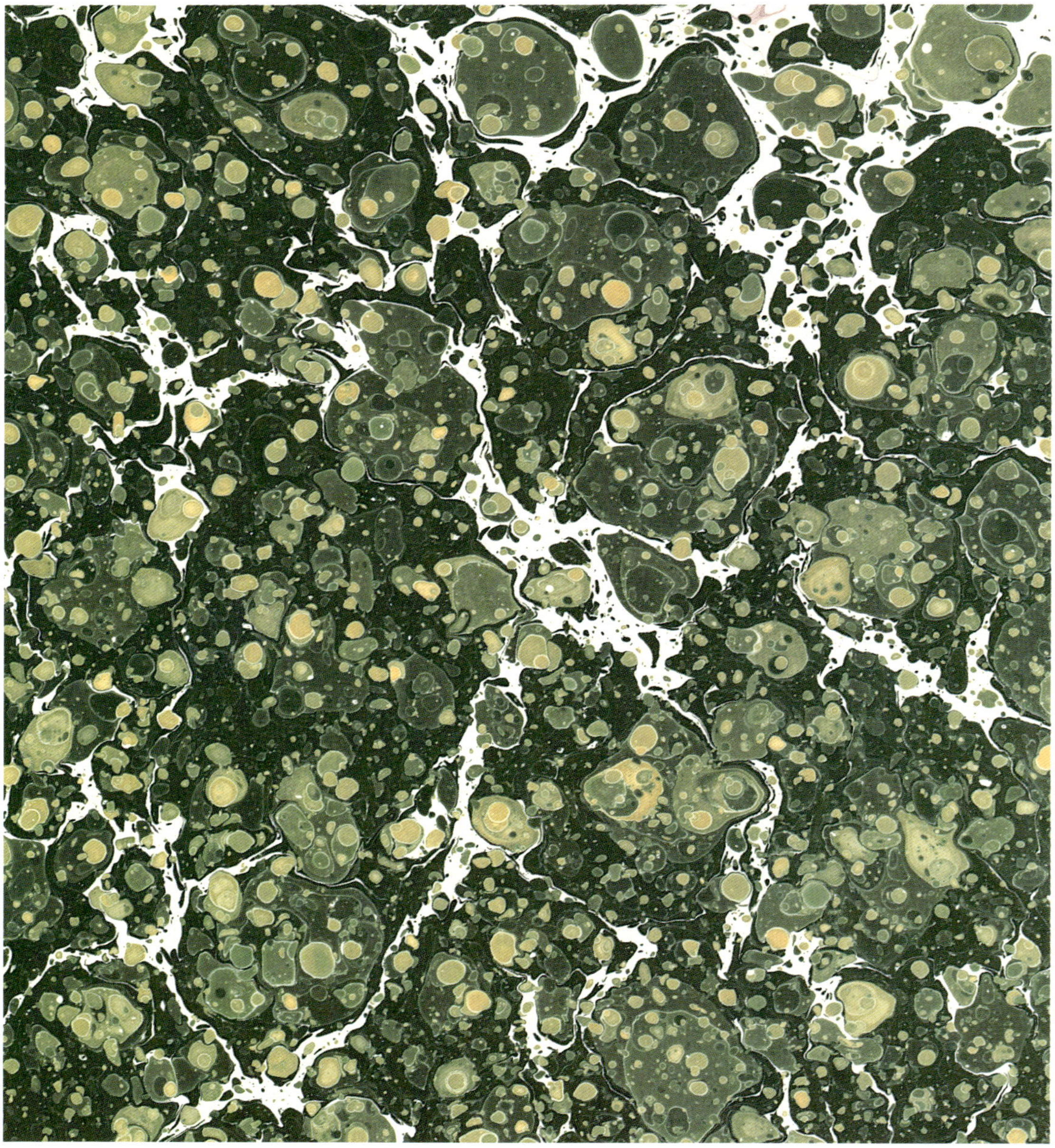

Freestyle Stone

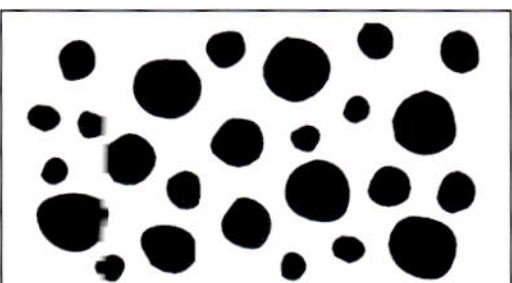

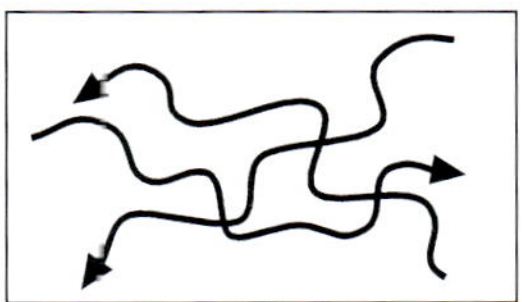

Draw a stylus through a Stone design in a wandering fashion.

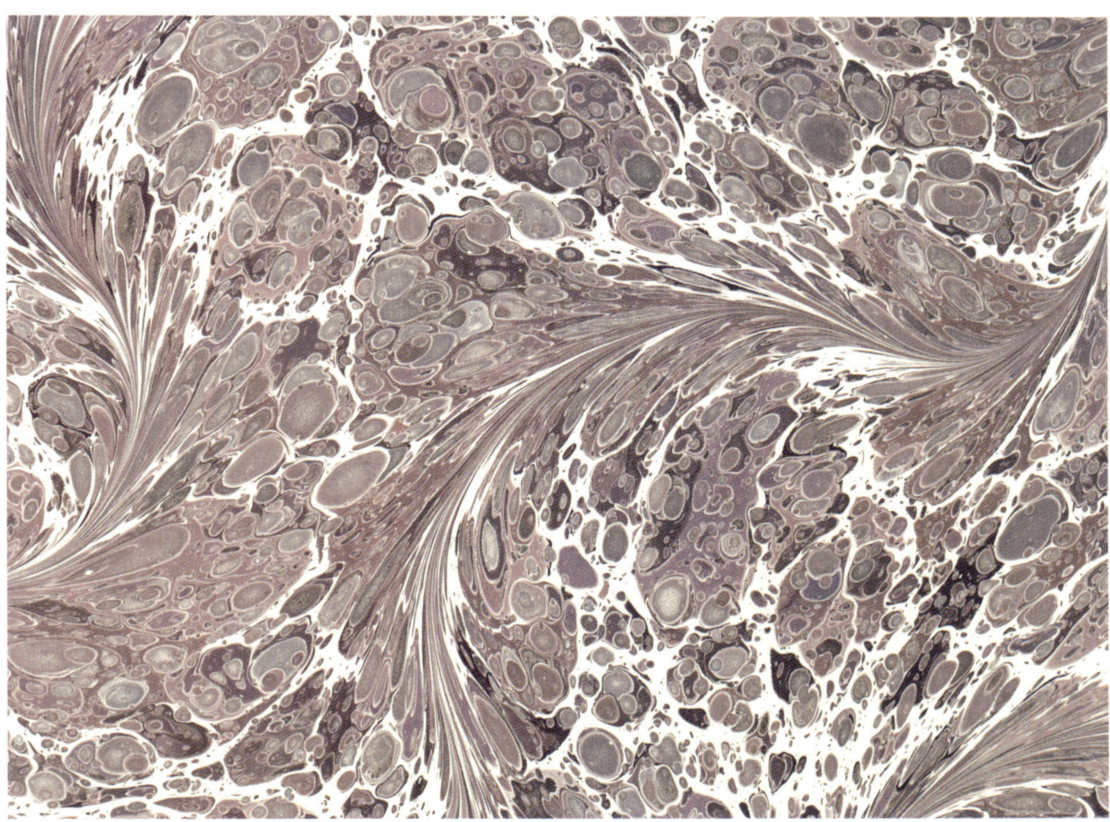

Snail

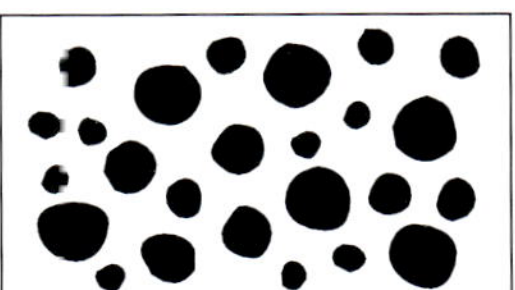

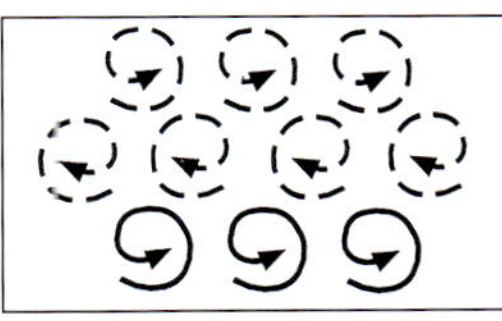

Make clockwise and counterclockwise spirals over a Stone or Rock pattern with a 3-inch (7.6-cm) rake. To make a tighter version of this pattern, use a 1-inch (2.5-cm) Bouquet comb. (The pattern shown here has been slightly reduced.)

PATTERNS BASED ON GEL GIT DESIGNS

Most combed designs are based on the Gel Git pattern. To start, use a whisk, eyedropper, dropper bottle, or brushes to apply a Stone or Rock pattern. Then follow the steps shown by Laura Crandall below to end up with a horizontal Gel Git pattern.

(Note: You may have seen the term *get gel* used in other marbling books. For years, this term was mistakenly used to refer to the traditional Turkish marbling design shown opposite. The correct term for this design is *gel git*, a Turkish phrase that means "back-and-forth.")

Horizontal Gel Git

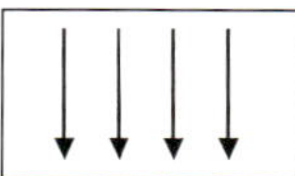

1. Draw a 3-inch (7.6-cm) rake toward you to begin breaking up and patterning the colors. (A rake with narrow teeth, such as this one, will create a bold design. A rake with thicker teeth will break up the color more to create a finer pattern.)

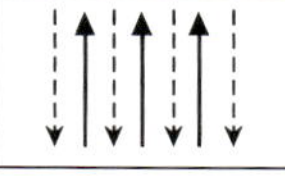

2. Without removing the rake from the size, move it over and push it away from you, bisecting the previous pass, to complete the initial vertical Gel Git.

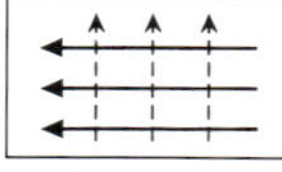

3. Rake horizontally, from right to left (or left to right, as shown above) to begin the horizontal Gel Git pattern.

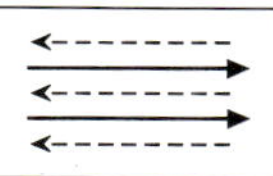

4. Rake in the opposite direction, bisecting the previous pass, to complete the horizontal Gel Git

Each set of opposing vertical or horizontal rake movements actually comprises a "gel git." The movements are done in pairs, so step 4 is technically a double Gel Git. (If you had begun by moving your rake in a horizontal direction, the final pattern would be comprised of vertical lines, and would be called a *vertical* Gel Git.)

The Gel Git movements break up and draw out the color droplets, allowing them to integrate with each other to create the lines of color upon which most patterns are built. Using a rake with thicker teeth will break up the color more, yielding finer lines and creating a more detailed pattern. A stylus can also be used to create this pattern, but the extra time it involves increases the risk of dust contamination.

Hor.zontal Gel Git pattern

Gel Git Curl

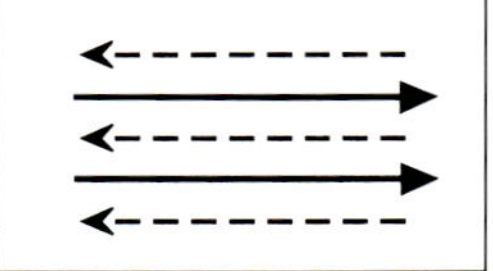

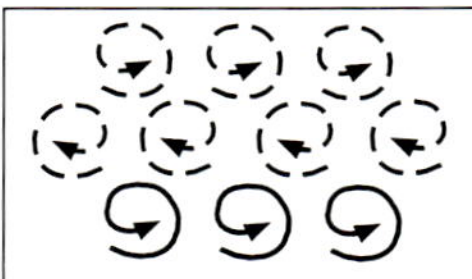

Use a $1\frac{1}{2}$-inch (3.8-cm) rake to make clockwise and counterclockwise spirals over a horizontal Gel Git pattern.

Zebra

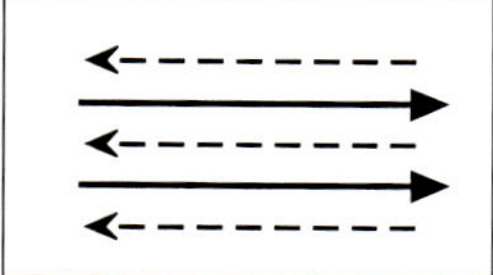

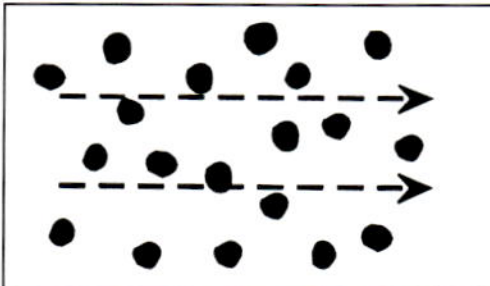

Use a whisk to apply a Stone pattern over a horizontal Gel Git pattern. The sample shown was made by applying a Stone pattern of diluted gall water, but you can also use color.

Peacock

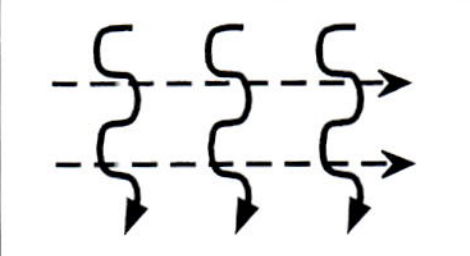

Create a horizontal Gel Git and then pull a 1-inch (2.5-cm) Bouquet comb toward you in short, curved waves. Practice to gain proficiency with this design. Some people find this easier to do if they think of the comb movement as a squared-off "S".

Cascade

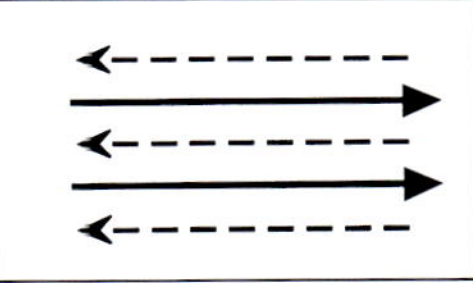

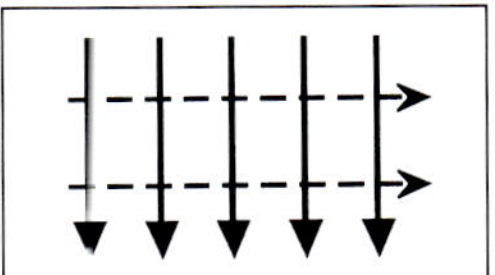

Pull a ½-inch (1.3-cm) comb toward you over a horizontal Gel Git.

American

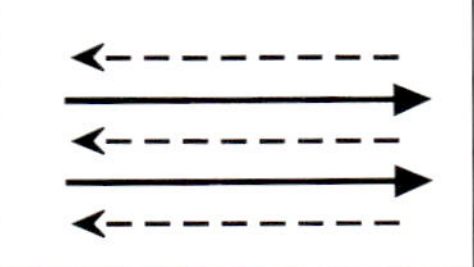

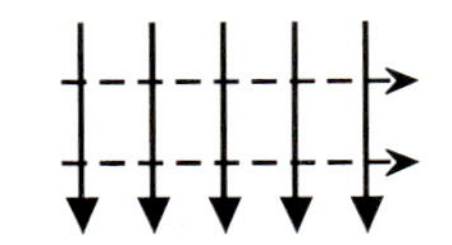

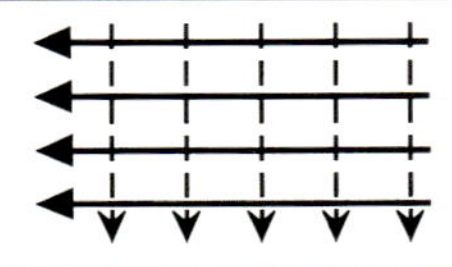

Pull a ½-inch (1.3-cm) comb from right to left over a Cascade pattern (see page 77).

PATTERNS BASED ON NONPAREIL DESIGNS

Nonpareil

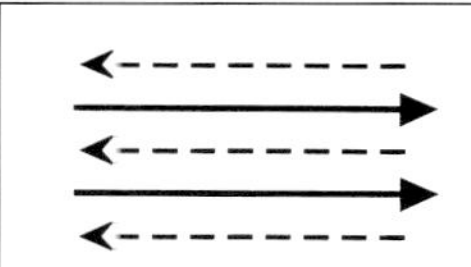

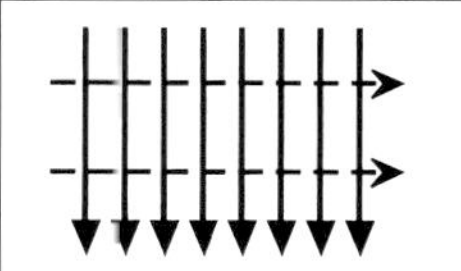

Pull a ¼-inch (0.6-cm) comb toward you over a horizontal Gel Git. To create a tighter Nonpareil pattern, use a ⅛-inch (0.3-cm) comb. A comb with a wider tooth spacing will give you the Cascade pattern (see page 77).

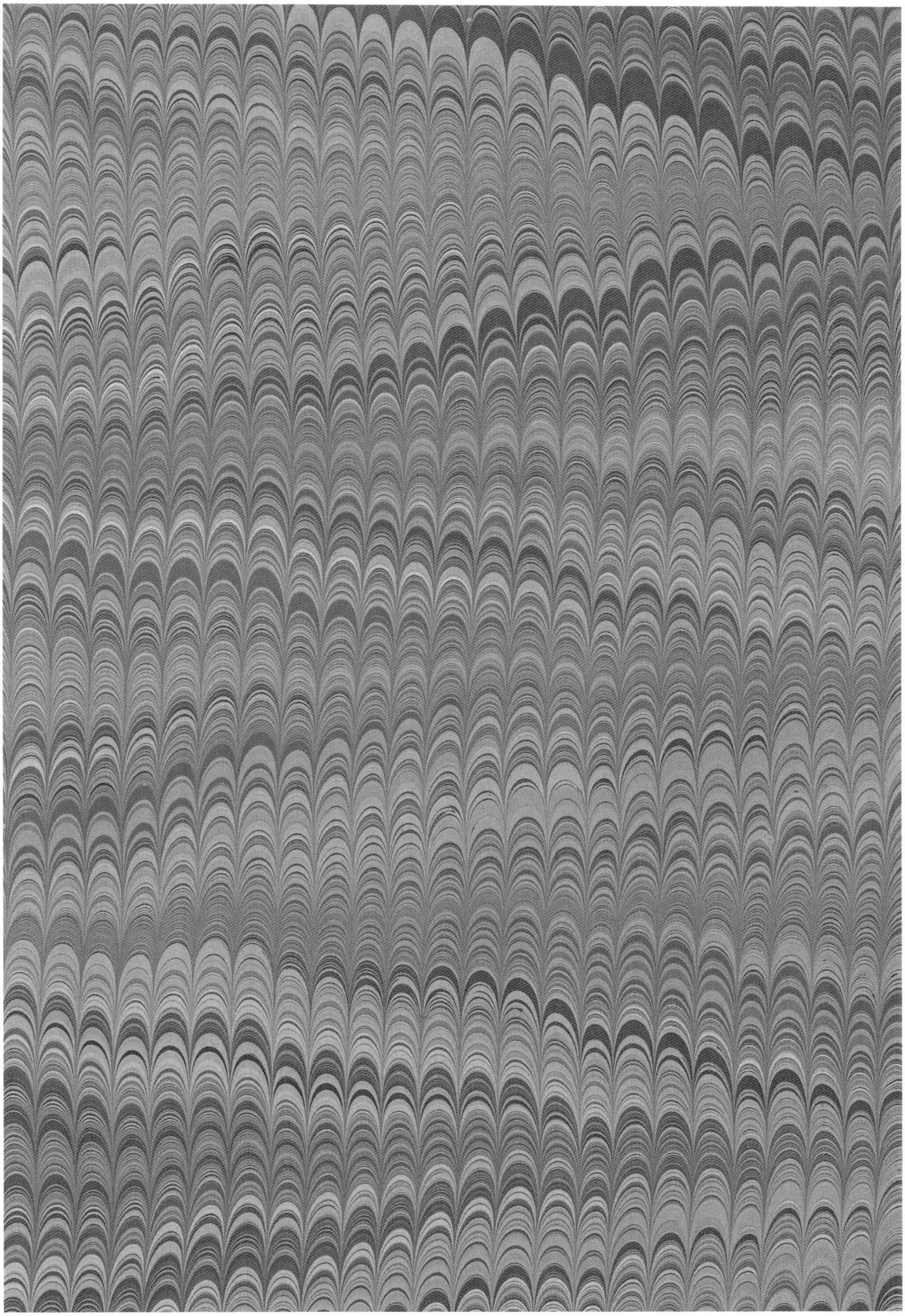

Double Nonpareil

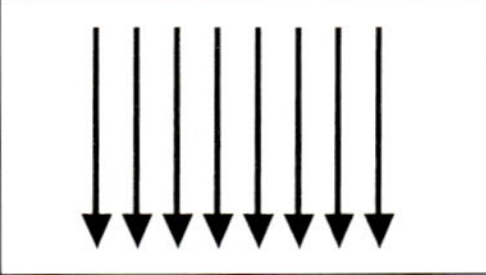

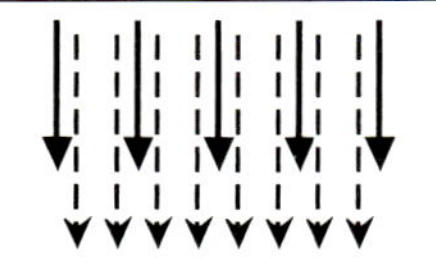

Draw a ½-inch (1.3-cm) comb toward you over a Nonpareil made with an ⅛-inch (0.3-cm) comb. (This is really a Cascade made over a tight Nonpareil.)

French Curl

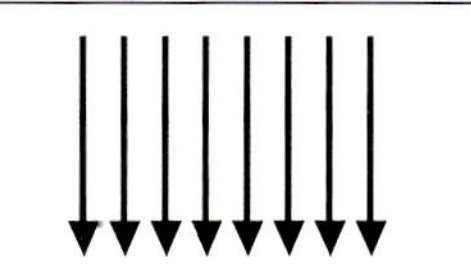

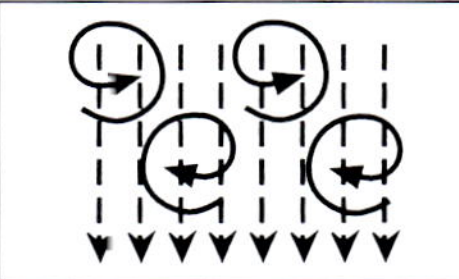

Use a 3-inch (7.6-cm) rake to create spirals over a Nonpareil design.

Pulled Nonpareil or Icarus

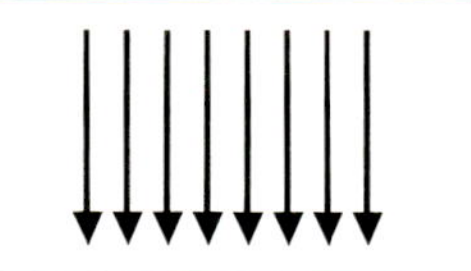

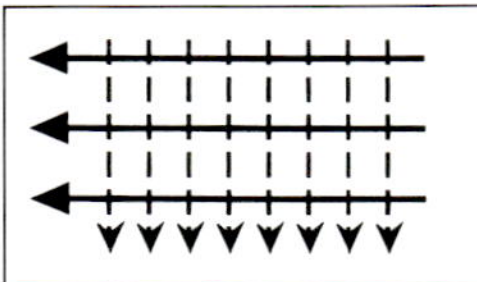

Pull a 1½-inch (3.8-cm) rake from right to left over a Nonpareil design.

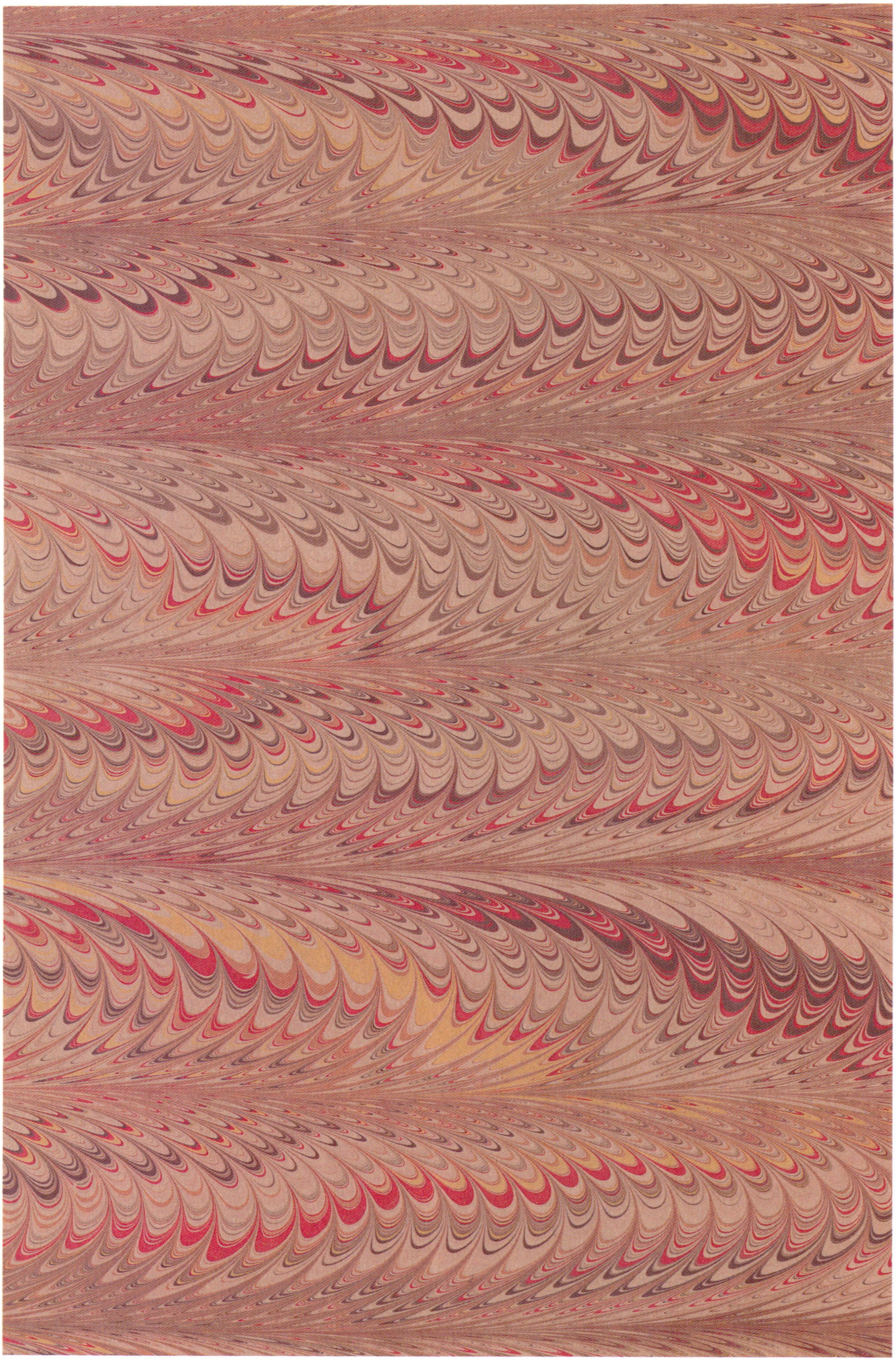

Waved Nonpareil or Waved Icarus

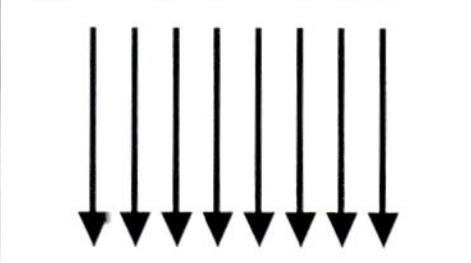

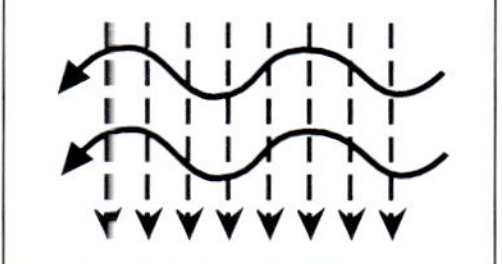

Wave a 3-inch (7.6-cm) rake from right to left over a Nonpareil design.

Dutch

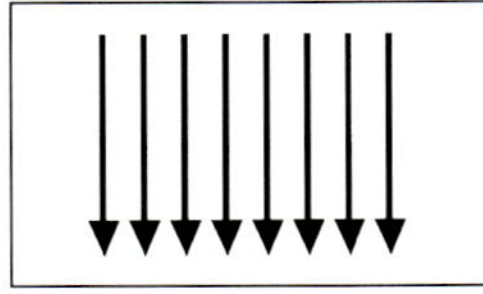

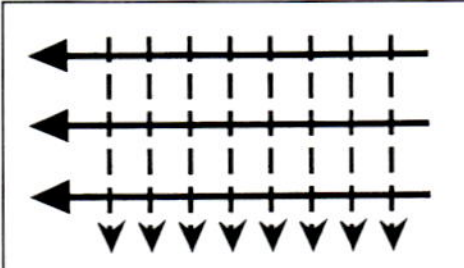

Pull a 1-inch (2.5-cm) comb from right to left over a Nonpareil design.

Fountain

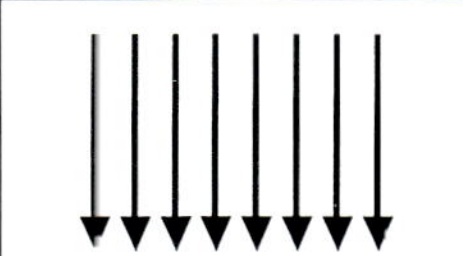

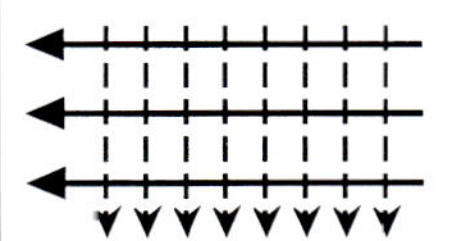

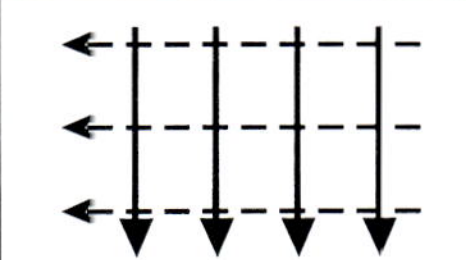

Pull a 2½-inch (6.4-cm) rake toward you over a Dutch pattern (see page 84).

Waved Dutch

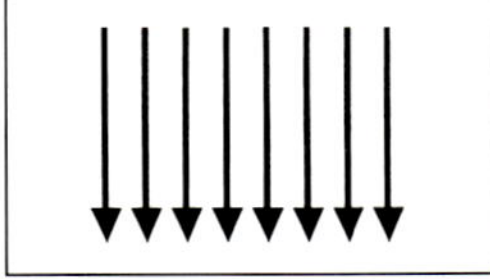

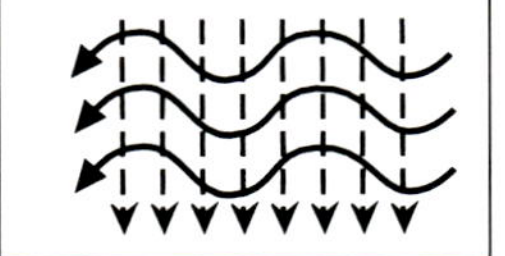

Wave a 1-inch (2.5-cm) comb from right to left over a Nonpareil design.

Feather

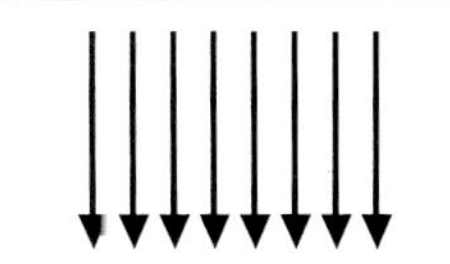

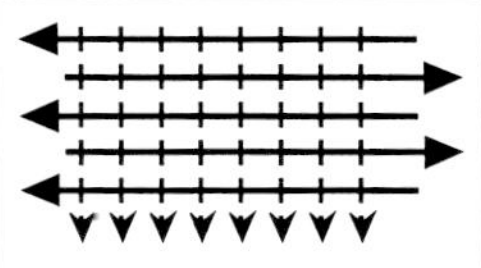

Draw a 1½-inch (3.8-cm) comb from right to left over a Nonpareil pattern. Then draw the comb from left to right, bisecting the previous pass.

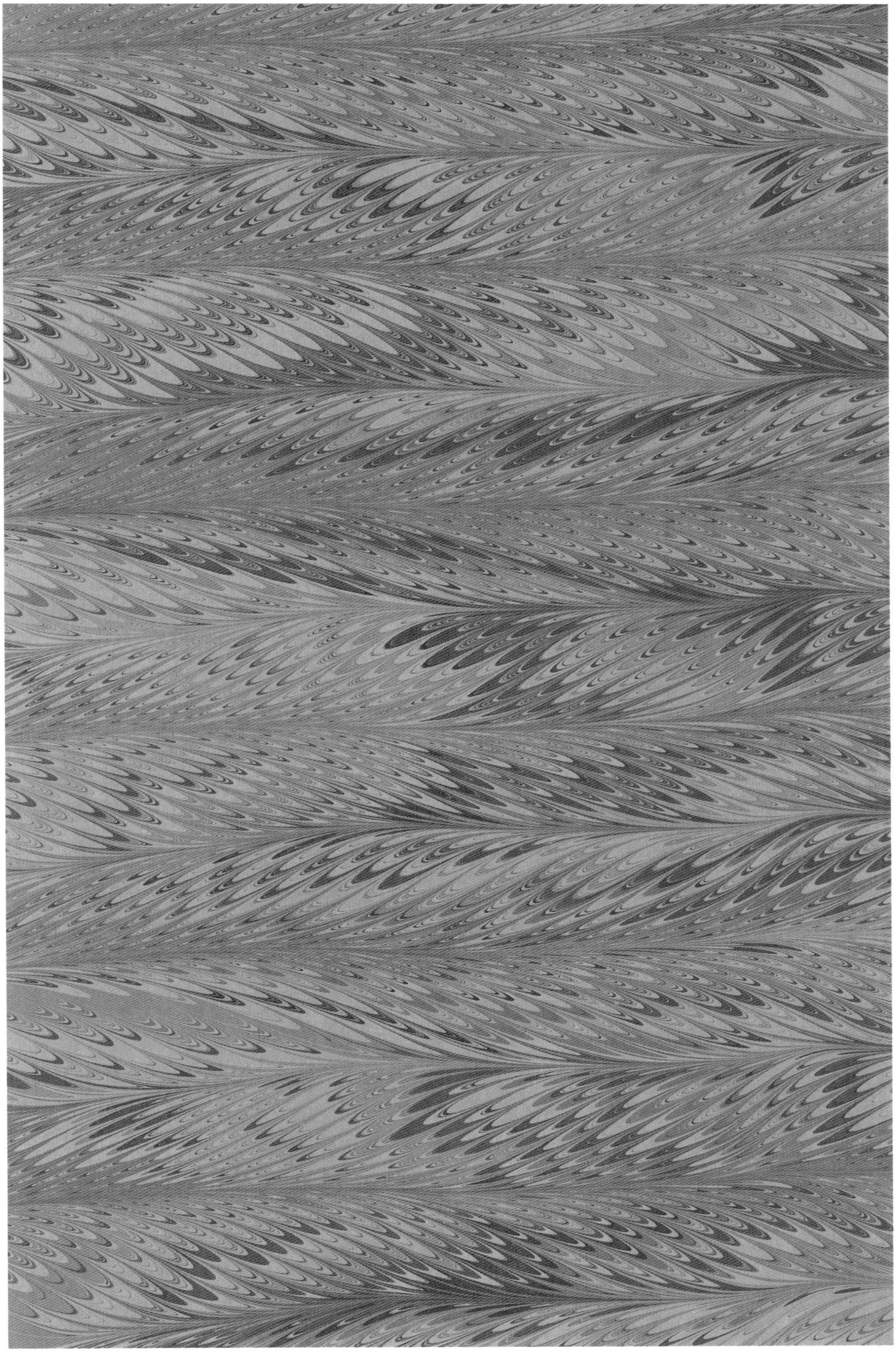

Waved Feather

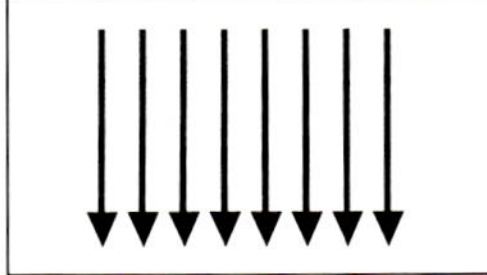

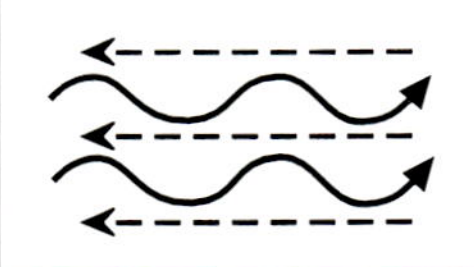

Draw a 1½-inch (3.8-cm) comb from right to left over a Nonpareil pattern. Then wave the comb gently while moving it from left to right, bisecting the previous pass.

Winged Nonpareil

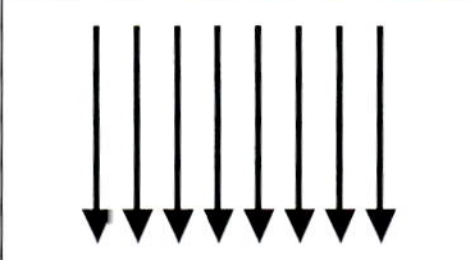

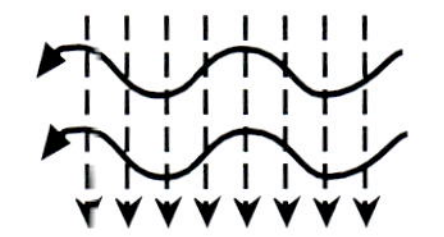

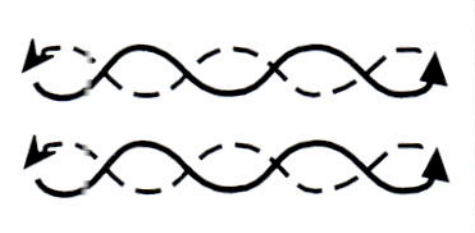

Wave a 3-inch (7.6-cm) rake from right to left and then from left to right, creating figure eights over a Nonpareil pattern.

Bouquet

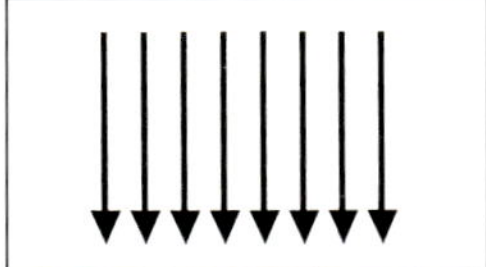

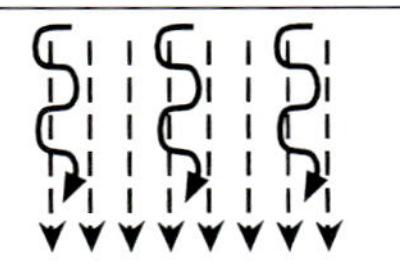

Slowly pull a 1-inch (2.5-cm) Bouquet comb toward you in squared-off "S"-shaped waves (as you did for Peacock, page 77) over a Nonpareil pattern.

Reverse Bouquet

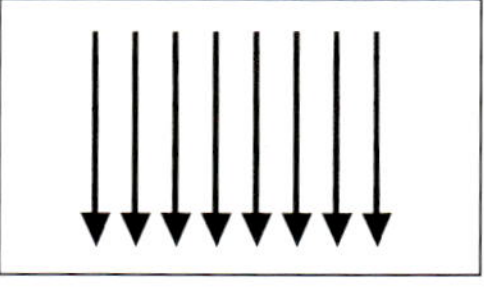

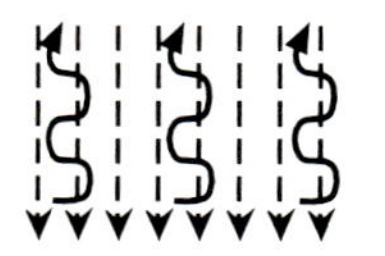

Push a 1-inch (2.5-cm) Bouquet comb away from you in "S"-shaped waves over a Nonpareil design.

Scallop

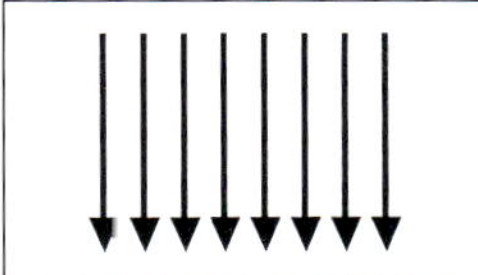

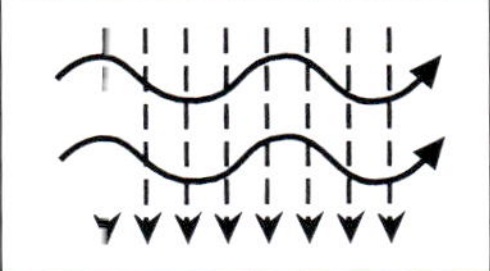

Wave a 1-inch (2.5-cm) Bouquet comb from left to right over a Nonpareil pattern. (The wave here is not as tight as for Bouquet, page 90.)

Waved Gothic

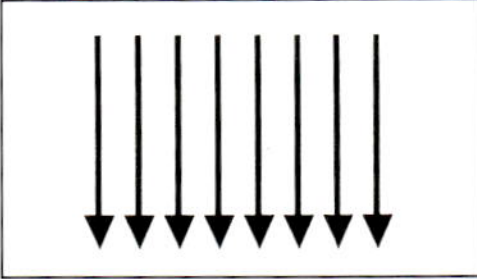

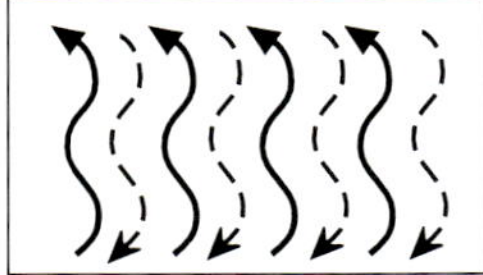

Pull a 3-inch (7.6-cm) rake toward you in a waved motion over an 1/8-inch (0.3-cm) Nonpareil. Then wave it away from you, bisecting the previous pass. Try to use a motion that parallels the first set of waves.

PATTERNS BASED ON CHEVRON DESIGNS

The Chevron is created like a vertical Gel Git with a ½- or ¾-inch (1.3- or 1.9-cm) comb. Because the first combing must be bisected exactly to produce the proper base for designs based on the Chevron, it is best to use a shallow or slightly thick size that will keep the pattern from wandering. I prefer to do this pattern by standing at the long side of the tray so that the sometimes difficult vertical Chevron extends only across the tray's width.

Vertical Chevron

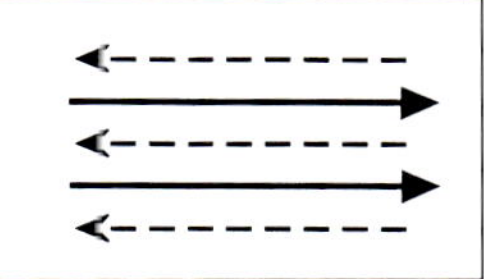

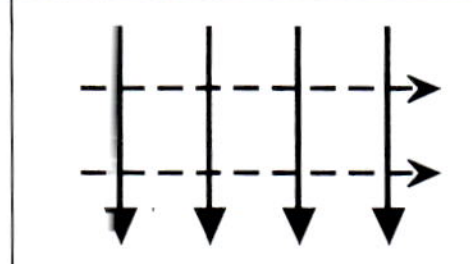

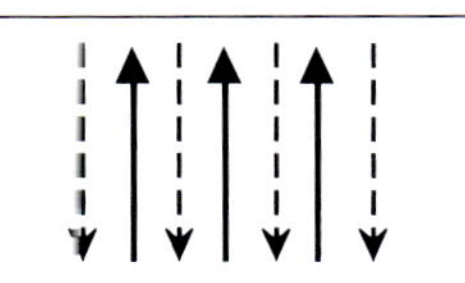

Create a horizontal Gel Git, then pull a ½-inch (1.3-cm) comb toward you to create the Cascade design. Push the comb away from you, bisecting the previous pass, to form a vertical Chevron.

Waved Chevron

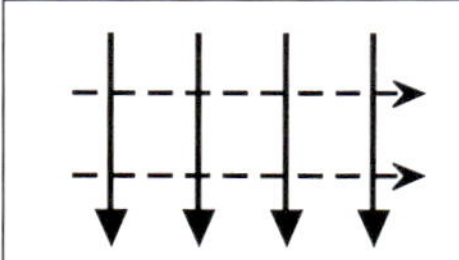

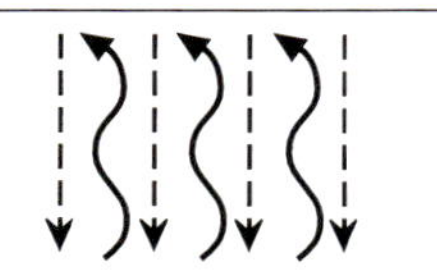

Create a horizontal Gel Git, then pull a ½-inch (1.3-cm) comb toward you to create the Cascade pattern (page 77). Wave the comb slightly as you push it away, bisecting the previous movement.

Palm or Fern

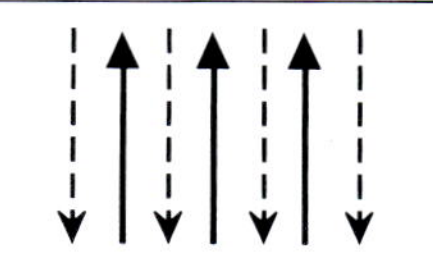

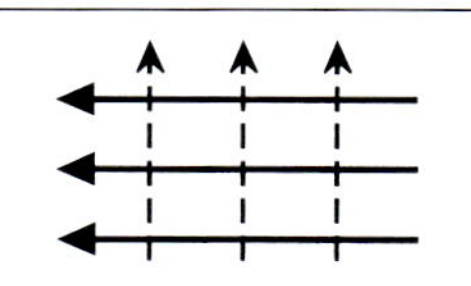

Pull a 2-inch (5.1-cm) rake from right to left across a vertical Chevron. Although it's easiest to create this pattern with a horizontal movement across the vertical Chevron, the final paper is usually shown in a vertical position (as this one is) so it resembles the palm for which it is named.

Flame or Chevron Waved Cross-Grain

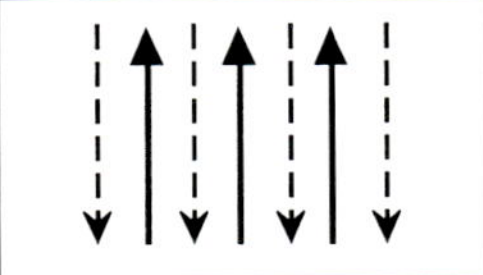

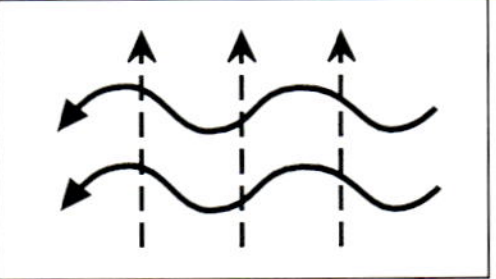

Wave a 1½-inch (3.8-cm) rake while moving it from right to left across a vertical Chevron.

Feathered Chevron

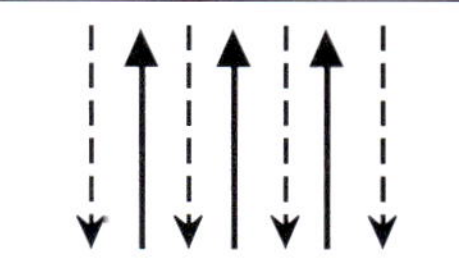

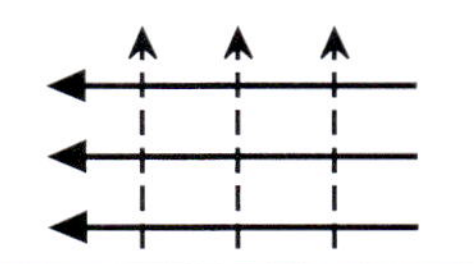

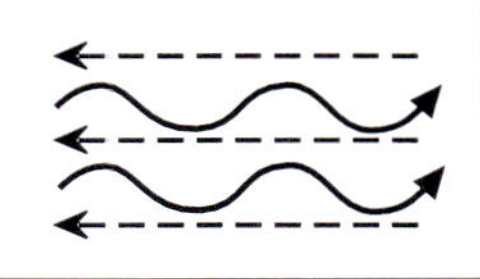

Move a 2½-inch (6.4-cm) rake from right to left across a vertical Chevron pattern. Then wave the rake from left to right, bisecting the previous movement.

Fleur-de-lis

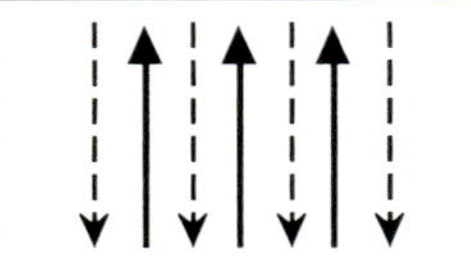

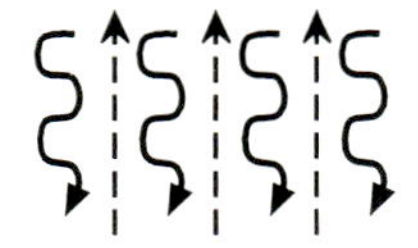

Pull a 1-inch (2.5-cm) Bouquet comb toward you in a shallow, elongated "S" movement over a vertical Chevron (following the grain of the Chevron).

Octopus

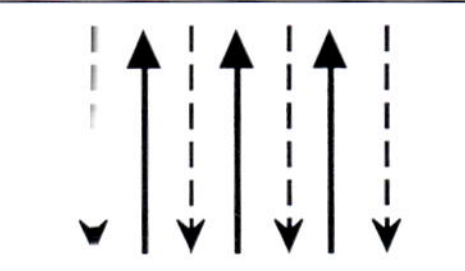

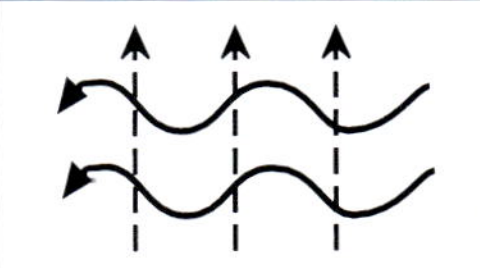

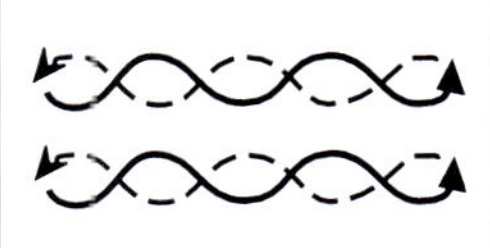

Wave a 3-inch (7.6-cm) rake from right to left across a vertical Chevron. Then wave the rake from left to right, creating a series of figure eights.

Altering the Image with Advanced Techniques

OVERMARBLING

Overmarbling, or multiple-image marbling, is a great way to save sheets that didn't quite turn out as planned. Often a rather homely paper can become the perfect underpainting for another design. Fine images can be patterned over bolder patterns, or vice versa. A tight or bold pattern created over an identical one, but offset or facing in the opposite direction, can be especially interesting.

When overmarbling, you needn't fill the tray with color for each layer. It can be more interesting to let images from various layers peek through to the next. If colors harmonize and successive patterns are progressively more translucent, up to six or more images can be successfully layered. Tom Leech, whose vibrant work is shown below, is a master of overmarbling. He explores all variations of layering images, including marbling over paintings, marbling over marbling, marbling over friskets, and painting over marbling.

To re-alum a sheet to be overmarbled, it's safest to place the sheet in a pan of alum water and then hang it to dry. Although I have successfully sponged alum water on marbled sheets, the initial image is sometimes disturbed in the process. If necessary, be sure to press and iron sheets to be remarbled. The more times a paper is rewetted, the more it tends to cockle, producing air bubble voids when you attempt to lay it on the size.

Marbled designs can also be layered over nonmarbled, printed papers with good results. Marbling over paste-paper designs or papers with a pattern of stripes (either printed on or painted on with a wide brush) or stamped images can also be effective. Using gall water to open areas of the marbled design will allow the printed paper to show through.

"In Xanadu" by Tom Leech, 18 x 24 inches (45.7 x 61 cm). Bold and fine patterns were layered to create this image.

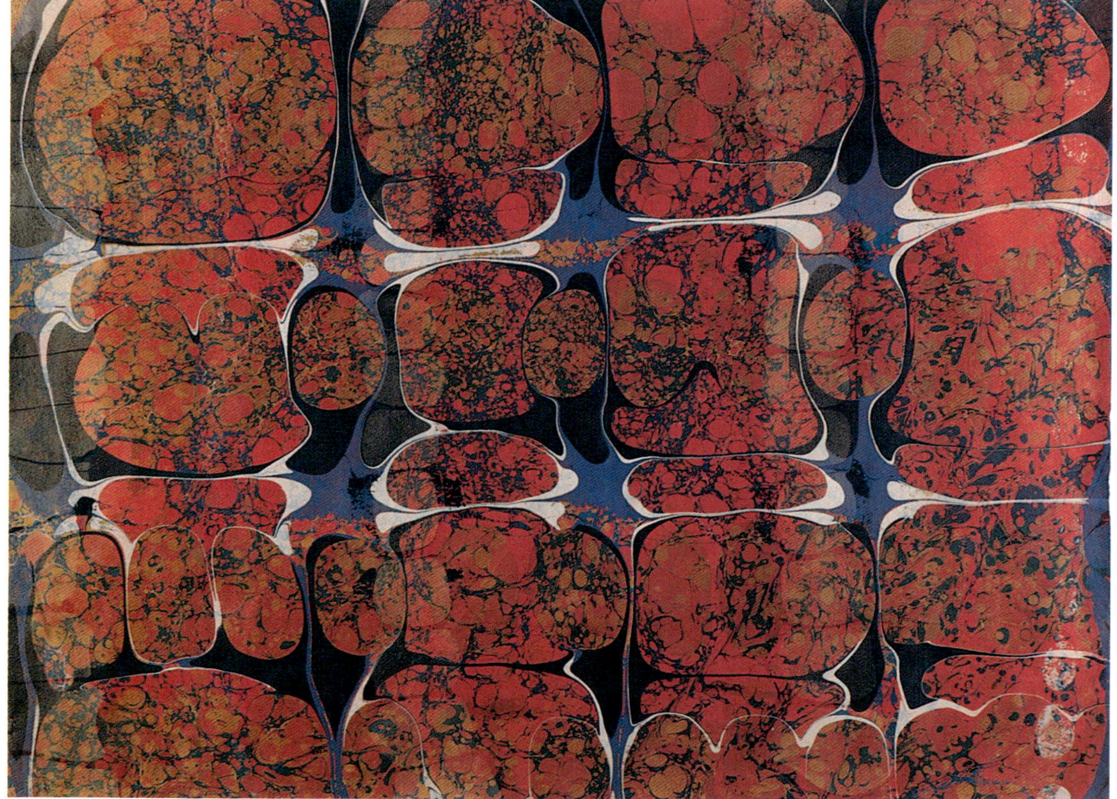

A double-image waved Chevron pattern by the author. Delicate designs were layered on top of each other in two separate printings.

To create this design, Iris Nevins painted diagonal stripes on a sheet of paper. Once the paper was dry, she alumed the sheet and then marbled over the stripes.

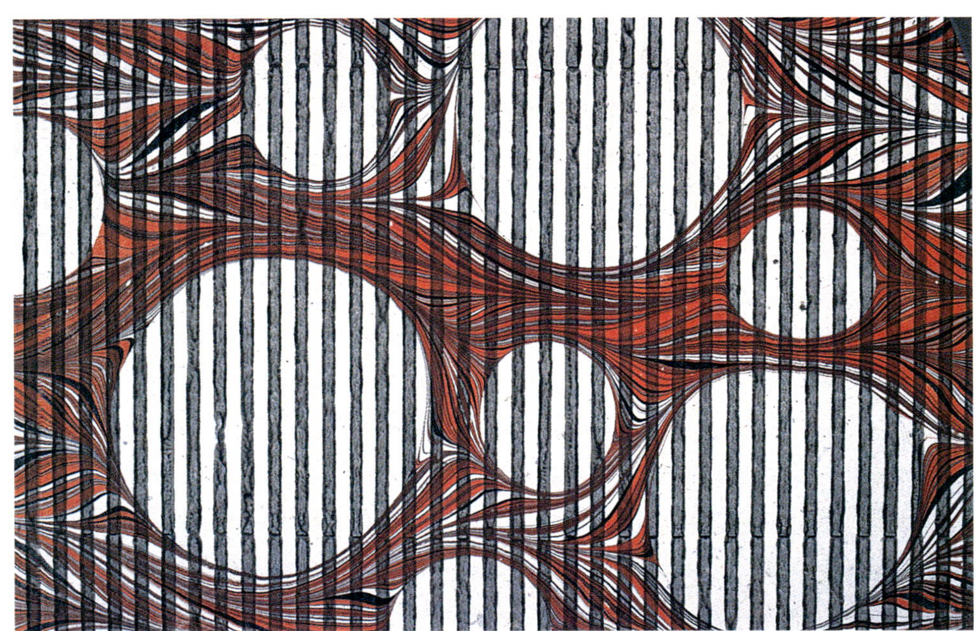

For this design, Mimi Schleicher used an eyedropper to deposit gall water over a marbled Gel Git pattern. The open areas that resulted allowed a printed striped paper to show through.

USING AN ATOMIZER TO CREATE SPECKLED DESIGNS

An artist's atomizer can be inserted into gall water or adjusted color and used to create fine misted or lacy effects, like those created by marbler Pam Smith (shown opposite). To use an atomizer correctly, first blow through both sections of it to make sure it's not clogged. Then open it completely to form an inverted "L," as shown below, and insert the small end into your adjusted color or gall water. (Try to work with at least ½ cup [120 ml] of color or gall water.) Direct the other end of the atomizer to a point several inches above the size surface. Take a deep breath and slowly blow through the mouthpiece opening to spray the color.

An atomizer in the open position. Mimi Schleicher produced the graphic background paper by using an atomizer to spray a fine mist of gall water over a ringed design.

Milena Hughes creating a balanced, geometric floral fantasy design

USING GALL WATER TO CREATE VOIDS AND RESTRICT COLOR SPREAD

As noted on page 68, gall water can be used to create open areas in multiple-image marbling. Depending upon the size of the openings you wish to create, the solution can be made weaker or stronger. For tiny holes placed here and there, a toothpick dipped in the solution may be a better applicator than an eyedropper.

Another way to use gall water is to apply it to the edges of a marbled pattern to squeeze the pattern in on itself. An allover Nonpareil design can be transformed into a thin, knarled tree trunk by applying gall water to selective parts of the marbled image. Dedree Drees has made some wonderful marbled tree paintings by using similar techniques (see opposite). Please note that some of the color may begin to sink as it is compressed, so it's necessary to work as quickly as possible.

Gall water applied to the perimeter or to certain areas of the marbling size will alter its surface tension and restrict the spread of colors applied. This can be especially useful when creating fantasy or flower marbling designs. Although a Stone pattern and the altered surface tension it creates is often the background for these designs, you may want the background to be the paper color only. Restricting the initial spread of the colors with gall water will give you smaller color drops that can then be teased into a design with a stylus. Milena Hughes, shown creating a fantasy design with a stylus (at left), uses this technique to create many of her intricate works.

USING SPRAY PAINT TO ACHIEVE MISTED EFFECTS

Susan Pogány sprays dry marbled papers with a light film of white spray paint. She then coats the papers with a fixative, re-alums them, and marbles them a second time to achieve a soft, misted look. She sometimes applies a mist of spray paint over a finished design to achieve an interesting, muted look (see opposite).

Detail of marbled sunflowers by Pam Smith. Pam used an atomizer to spray color on top of her flowers, producing a delicate, allover speckled design.

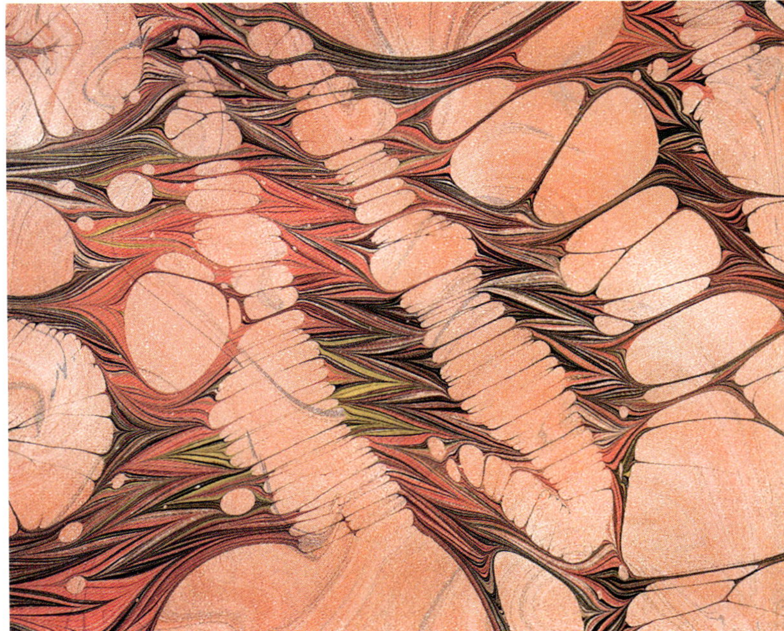

This piece by Susan Pogány was overmarbled and misted with spray paint.

"Tree-Winter" by Dedree Drees, 23 x 18 inches (58.4 x 45.7 cm). Dedree used gall water to compress parts of the marbling and coax it into this striking image.

USING TRADITIONAL PAINT ADDITIVES

FRENCH SHELL

A marbled pattern known as French Shell, popular in Europe and the United States during the early nineteenth century, is created by making a Stone pattern with a whisk and adding a tiny drop of olive oil to the last color applied. (Just dip a wooden toothpick in olive oil and touch it to about 1/4 cup [60 ml] of color.) When this color is stirred and tapped from the whisk, it forms shapes with an almost three-dimensional halo, formed by a lighter ring of color. The pattern is both lovely and historically correct, but olive oil will contaminate your tray, whisk, and color, making it impossible to create any other patterns until everything has been carefully cleaned with rubbing alcohol and hot water.

Iris Nevins, who specializes in duplicating historic patterns, discovered that by adding a tiny drop of gum turpentine to the last color applied she could create a fine French Shell without contaminating her equipment (see below, left). (Because turpentine evaporates quickly, it disappears from your tools and size within minutes.) To create a pattern of tiny shells, she adds turpentine to the last two or even three colors applied. She cautions that because turpentine is a dispersant, you may want to add little or no gall to these colors when mixing them. (You may be able to acheive a pattern very similar to French Shell, but without adding any oil or turpentine, by applying a Stone pattern and continuing to tap the almost-dry whisk.)

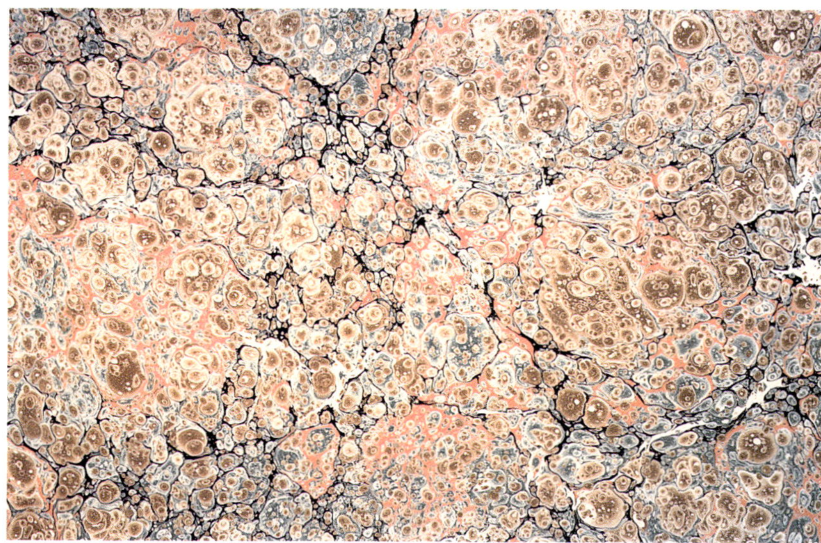

A French Shell design by Iris Nevins

STORMONT

This pattern is made by adding two drops of turpentine to the last color applied to a Stone pattern. The additional turpentine will make the paint spread a bit more than in a French Shell, and will also create holes in the pattern (see below).

A Stormont pattern by Iris Nevins

GLOSTER

This design is made by first creating a Gel Git pattern and then using a whisk to apply color mixed with two drops of turpentine over the pattern (see below). The lines of color will become increasingly disturbed and compressed as you add more and more turpentine to the last color applied. (Note: Because turpentine evaporates, you may have to periodically adjust the paint-turpentine mixture as you marble.)

ITALIAN HAIR VEIN

To create this classical design, first apply a Stone pattern with a whisk. Then mix a solution of 1 tablespoon (15 ml) spirits of soap and ⅔ cup (160 ml) of water. When sprinkled over the Stone pattern, the soap solution will push the design into tight veins of color (see below). Gall water can also be used to create a similar pattern. In either case, be sure to thoroughly rinse all soap or gall out of your whisk before inserting it into a color.

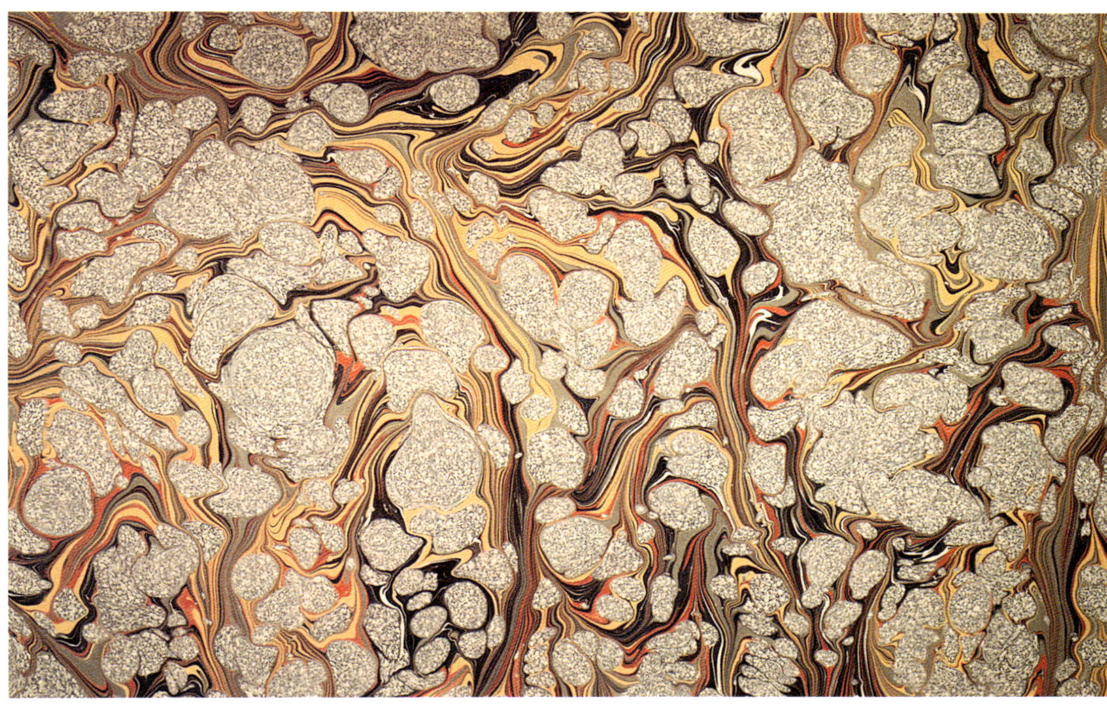

A Gloster pattern by Iris Nevins. A Gel Git pattern was the starting point for this design.

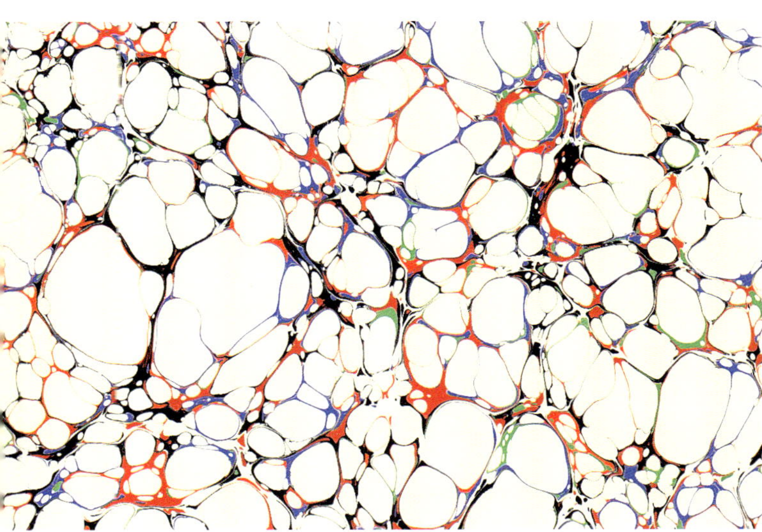

An Italian Hair Vein pattern created with a whisk by Mimi Schleicher

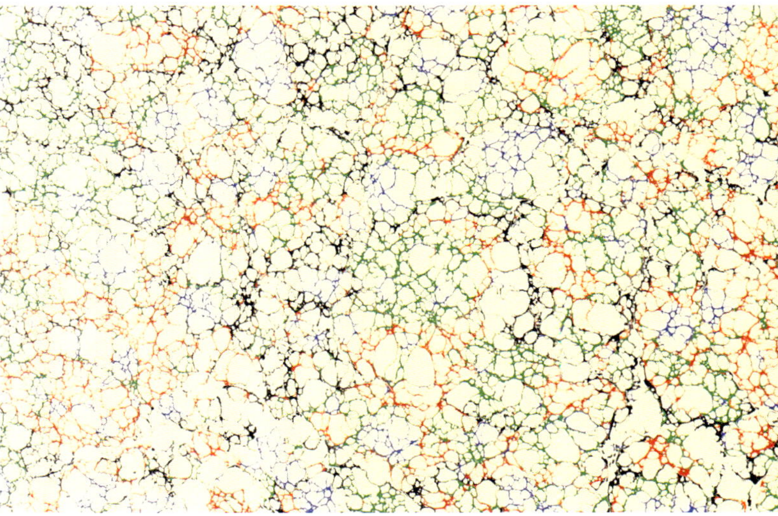

Mimi used an atomizer to create this tighter version of an Italian Hair Vein.

KUMLU

This grainy or sandy pattern is commonly used by Turkish marblers, and can be seen in the work of Christopher Weimann on page 112. It can be achieved by adding a pinch of alum to colors before they are applied to the size. Adding alcohol to colors can sometimes produce the same effect.

TIGER EYE

More than a few marblers have been frustrated trying to create the marbled design known as Tiger Eye, or Sun-Ray. The spots of color—which radiate in progressively lighter colors from a dark center—look like eyes or lovely ruffled flowers, depending on their size. The recipe for Tiger Eye has been around for ages, but most marblers who try it find that something seems to have been left out. Either the eyes don't form at all, they break apart, or they form and then slide off the paper during rinsing. The chemical composition of colors used to create the background pattern seems to influence the design considerably, as does the surface tension of the size.

Eva van Breugel, an exceptional Dutch marbler, produced the gorgeous Tiger Eye pattern shown here (below, left). She began her design with a heavily pigmented paint prepared for the Stormont design, to which she'd added a drop of sunflower oil. Unhappy with the Stormont she achieved, Eva added an additional drop of turpentine to the color. On a whim, she then took a "pinch of soda crystals, a pinch of potash, and a sniff of alum crystals" and added them to the leftover Stormont paint, stirring the mixture until all ingredients dissolved. When thrown as the third or fourth color on a thin marbling size, the well-formed Tiger Eyes appeared.

While experimenting with Tiger Eye recipes and lacking the ingredient potash, Iris Nevins tried woodstove ash instead. She was rewarded with the unusual ruffled images shown below. (The woodstove ash, however, creates some unusually dusty conditions.)

While stalking the Tiger Eye, Iris Nevins created this unusual design with woodstove ash.

Eva van Breugel's stunning Tiger Eye paper

INDIGO EYE

Sometimes the natural chemistry of a particular color lends itself to the creation of amazing designs. Turkish marbler Beki Almaleh has developed a way of using Lahor Blue, a fine indigo imported from India, to create the Indigo Eye shown here (below, left). To use the stonelike Lahor Blue, Beki dissolves a piece the size of a sugar lump in ½ cup (120 ml) of distilled water. The paint crackles as it dissolves into a creamy consistency, and is ready for use after the addition of a drop of ox gall. To make the eye, Beki first applies a pattern with conventional colors on a rather thin size. She then uses an eyedropper to deposit a drop of the Lahor Blue. Next comes a drop of gall water for the white of the eye, some yellow paint, and a final drop of Lahor Blue for the eye's pupil.

The textures and mosslike projections in this pattern vary with the consistency of the size, the quality of the Lahor Blue, and the whims of the marbling muse. As with so many other special techniques, these effects are easy to achieve on some days and impossible on others.

USING INCOMPATIBLE PAINTS OR SOURED PAINT

Rather than discarding them, save moldy, sour, or grainy paints for experimental use. Some paints that freeze during shipment, for example, often become very grainy or separate into beads and little globules of color when you begin to comb them. One particular turquoise paint produced in England was prone to this problem and, as a marbling supplier, I heard many complaints about the color. When the company stopped making the faulty turquoise, however, I began hearing moans of sorrow because many marblers had finally discovered the novel designs it made and now prized the ornery paint!

When mixed together, paints with incompatible chemistry can also create interesting designs. The design pictured (below, right) was formed by mixing gouache-based paints produced by different marbling suppliers. Try mixing gouache colors with pigmented drawing inks, or Holbein iridescent gouache colors with marbling watercolors.

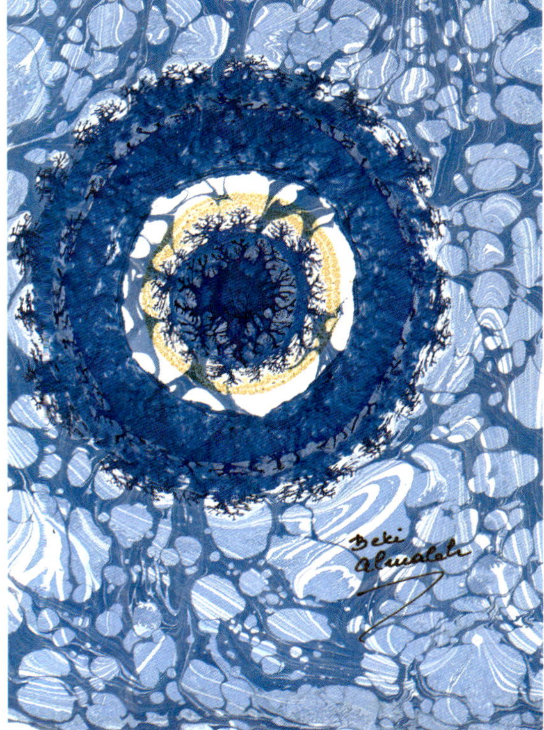

Beki Almaleh used a special type of indigo paint to create her "Indigo Eyes," 6¾ x 4¾ inches (17.1 x 12.1 cm).

Two incompatible brands of watercolor paints produced the rippled edges of "Strata," by the author, 10⅝ x 7⅛ inches (27 x 18.2 cm). One of these brands, unfortunately, is no longer made

USING NONTRADITIONAL PAINT ADDITIVES

Ingredients found in cosmetics, cleaning products, pharmaceuticals, and foods can make watercolor marbling colors behave in novel ways. Rummage through your pantry, medicine chest, and basement shelves for potions and elixirs to see how they will affect your watercolor-marbled designs. If other household members question your actions and mad-scientist demeanor, explain that there's historical precedent for your behavior: early European marblers tried various oil and spirit additives in their marbling, and we modern-day marblers have many more ingredients to choose from! Just be sure to try experiments at the end of the day as they are sure to pollute your size and colors.

Here are a few ideas to get you started:

"Bondurant's Snowflake" (below, left), a design discovered by Mary B. Warren and created by Mimi Schleicher, was made by sprinkling a mixture of one part egg white to seven parts water over a blue Stone pattern.

Paul Maurer added shoe polish to watercolor marbling paints to create the unusual overmarbled design pictured here (below, right). The marbling size was thin and old, which helped to distort the Nonpareil part of the design.

To create her Gel Git flocked paper (opposite, top), Mimi Schleicher applied color, followed by a weak solution of alum water and ox gall, followed by more color.

To create the brown speckled background in the work pictured (opposite, middle), Susan Pogány sprayed Parmatex, a brand of silicone spray lubricant, over the floating color.

To create the black and white weblike design shown here (opposite, bottom), Susan sprayed Aqua Net hair spray over the applied color.

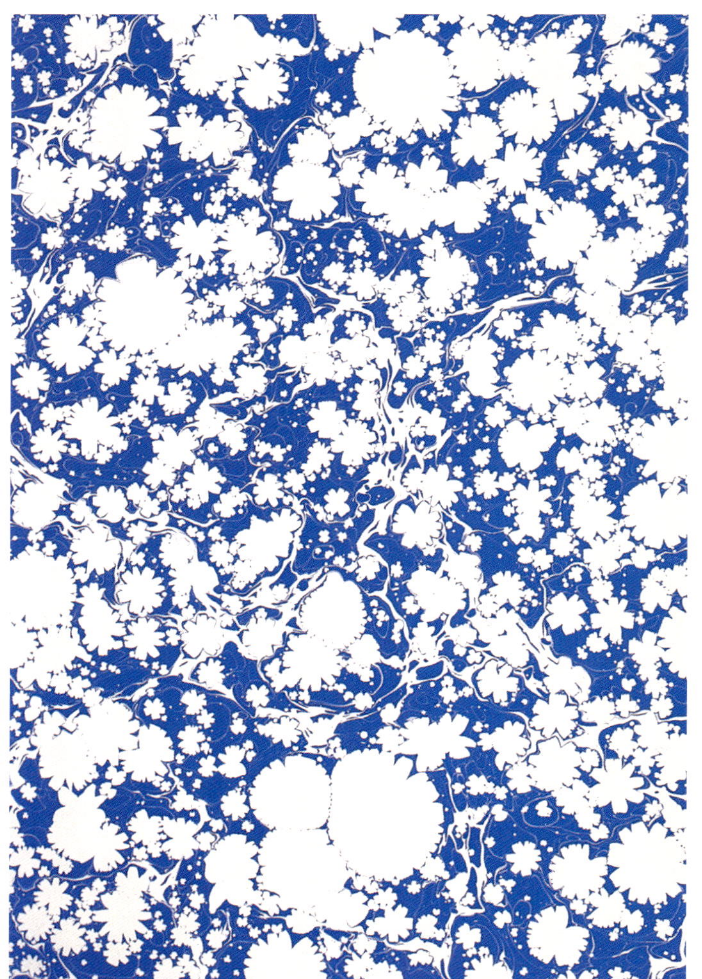

Detail of "Bondurant's Snowflake" by Mimi Schleicher and Mary B. Warren, 18 x 12 inches (45.7 x 30.5 cm)

Paul Maurer added shoe polish to marbling paints to produce this overmarbled design.

Mimi Schleicher used a weak solution of alum and water with some ox gall in it to create this flocked paper.

Susan Pogány used a silicone spray over floating color to produce this work. She warns that the spray quickly contaminates the marbling size.

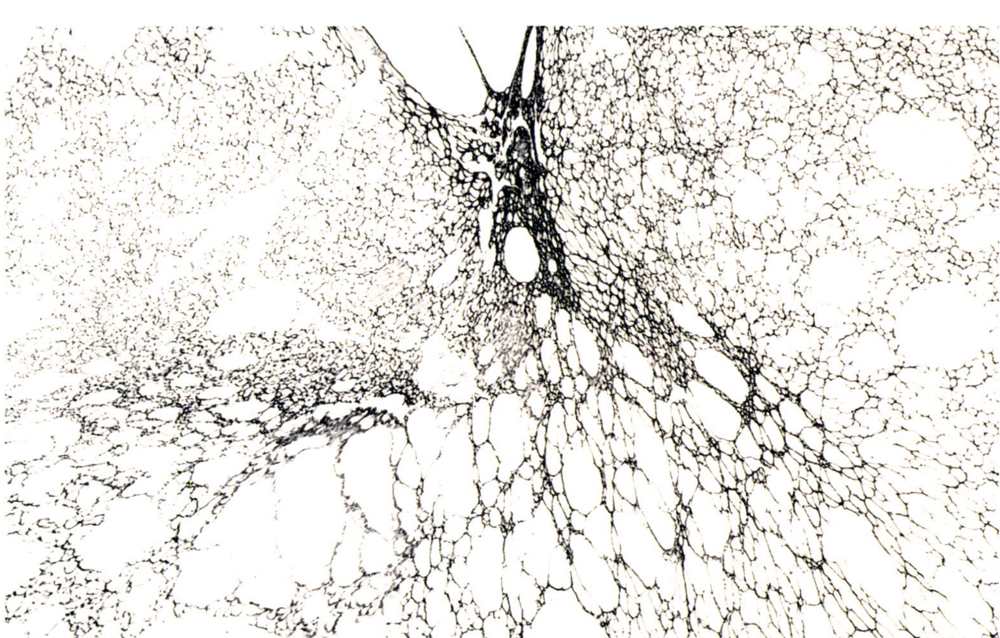

Aqua Net hair spray propelled Susan Pogány's Stone marbling into this webbed design.

COMPRESSING AND EXPANDING COMBED COLORS

Marie Palowoda shares an interesting method for making designs she calls "Lace Agate." First, Marie creates an acrylic Gel Git pattern in a small tray. After the pattern is created, Marie uses a strip of newspaper to "skim" the color to one side of the tray, compressing the design. She then releases the strip and skims the color toward the opposite side of the tray, compressing it again. When she releases the skim strip the second time, lacy patterns (like those pictured) often result. She cautions that dry, warm conditions are necessary for this technique to work successfully.

For other examples of color-compression marbling techniques, see the work of Milena Hughes on pages 131–132, the vibrant work of Susan Pogány on page 138, and the work of Turkish marbler Hikmet Barutcugil on page 46.

Marie compressing her design by skimming it to one side of the tray

An example of Marie's "Lace Agate" design

USING FRISKETS AND MASKS

Liquid frisket and frisket film, as discussed in the chapters on suminagashi and oil color marbling (see pages 25 and 43), can also be used in watercolor marbling. Liquid frisket can be diluted for artful splattering, or used full strength to preserve unmarbled designs or lettering on a sheet of paper. Galen Berry created "Jeff," pictured opposite, by applying liquid frisket with a calligraphy pen. Because the aluming process can disturb the liquid frisket, it's safest to alum the paper before applying the liquid frisket. When the print is thoroughly dry, you can peel the frisket off.

Frisket film can be used to mask out larger areas, enabling marblers to create complicated overmarbled pieces (see "The Crucible," page 136 and "Buck," page 141). When marbling with frisket film, you can alum the paper after the film is applied. Instead of frisket film, Galen often uses Scotch Removable Tape with good results.

If you wish to mask out a very simple shape, you may be able to use a piggyback frisket. A piggyback frisket is cut from acetate or water-proofed paper and affixed with surgeon's tape to the sheet of paper before it's marbled. (Piggy-back friskets are not generally used for suminagashi or oil color marbling.) The advantage of this type of frisket is that it can be reused. The disadvantage is that, because it's not held as securely in place, it might show fuzzy edges where some color migration occurred.

To use a piggyback frisket, make several small rings of tape, adhesive-side out, and place them on the back of a cut-out design. Press this new frisket in place on the sheet to be marbled, taking special care to flatten the edges, under which color could seep. When you're sure the edges are down, alum the paper and attached frisket, then marble as usual. Remove the frisket while rinsing and use a soft brush to coax off any color that has seeped under its edges. Clean, dry, and press the frisket before using it to make another print.

Although more difficult to use successfully, floating friskets may also be used to mask out areas of watercolor-marbled designs. I frankly wouldn't have believed it if Tom Leech hadn't sent me his "Making Paper in *A Flat*," an overmarbled piece created with an unattached floating frisket (shown below). To use a floating frisket, pattern your colors, apply the floating friskets, and lay the paper (quickly!).

Galen Berry applied liquid frisket with a calligraphy pen to mask out the word "Jeff" before marbling this paper.

"Making Paper in A Flat*" by Tom Leech, 18 x 24 inches (45.7 x 61 cm). Tom created this intricate multiple-image work (whose title refers to a musical note) by floating friskets on the size and then applying the paper to be marbled.*

Christopher Weimann holding the first stage of his replication of the seventeenth-century marbled painting "A Female Devotee in Prayer" (the original is shown on page 11). This photo shows the positive stencil glued in place with most of the gum resist brushed on.

Christopher's replica after the gum resist and sandy Kumlu pattern had been completed

USING STENCILS AND RESISTS

A more complicated type of stencil resist can be cut from acetate or wax-saturated paper and glued in place with a water-soluble glue on the sheet to be marbled. Both positive cut-outs and the negative designs formed by their removal can be used as stencils. When stencils are used, the marbled print is placed in a pan of water for rinsing. This helps dissolve the glue and allows the stencil to be gently peeled off.

Christopher Weimann, whose untimely death in 1988 was a loss to the marbling world, was a master of marbling and working with stencil resists. He spent much time creating replicas of seventeenth-century marbled paintings, and researching the multilayered resist and stencilled designs of ancient Indian paintings. The photographs shown here are of Chris working with resists and stencils.

To create a replica of "A Female Devotee in Prayer," pictured on page 11, Chris first cut stencils to mask the figure and other areas to be filled with a marbled pattern. He then positioned the positive stencils on the paper, gluing and pressing them into place. Next, he brushed a dark gum resist in horizontal lines across the part of the paper not covered by the stencils. When the resist was dry, Chris marbled the paper in a sandy Kumlu pattern (see page 106 for a description of this pattern). The figure and foliage, still covered by stencils, remained uncolored.

Chris then soaked the paper and removed the stencils. After waiting for the work to dry, he recoated it with alum. Next, he cut the negative background stencil and glued it into place, preserving the areas marbled with the Kumlu pattern. With the female figure and foliage exposed, and the rest of the painting still masked off, Chris marbled the paper in a tarakli-ebru (Nonpareil) design to produce the fine marbled figure. Finally, after removing all stencils and resists, he completed the marbled painting by drawing in the head, hands, and gold detailing.

Christopher cutting the background stencil for the second stage of the work

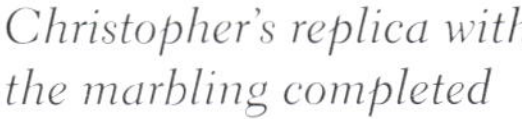

Christopher's replica with the marbling completed

CREATING SHIFTED DESIGNS

To make beautiful waved and shaded watercolor-marbled patterns, follow the shifting experiments and Spanish marbling techniques outlined for oil color marbling (see page 50). The designs can be made over various Stone or combed patterns.

If you find the hand movements for Spanish marbling impossible to coordinate, try keeping your hands steady and rocking your body back and forth as you lay down the sheet to be marbled. Your movements will transfer to the paper and alternately push the colors together and pull them back to create a series of dark and light diagonal waves of color. As mentioned before, Spanish marbling takes a lot of patience and practice to master. It's best accomplished on a fresh and rather thick size.

Susan Pogány began this Spanish marbled work by creating a Gel Git pattern. By not filling her entire tray with color, she isolated the design, framing it with the rich paper color, to create an exciting composition.

FOLDING THE PAPER TO CREATE A SPANISH MOIRE DESIGN

This is one of the most difficult shifted patterns to create and cause for a night on the town when successfully executed. The undulating waves and curved lines of shaded color in Spanish Moire may be easier to produce if you first become proficient with regular Spanish marbling.

To attempt this pattern, take a dry sheet of alumed paper and lay it on a board, alum-side down. Roll the paper into about a 3-inch (7.6-cm) tube and, with the tube still lying horizontally on the board, *gently* press down to flatten it without making a hard fold. Then, still keeping the paper alum-side down, open it and give it a quarter turn so that it faces the opposite direction. Again, roll it up and use your arms to gently flatten the paper. When unrolled, your sheet should now show a series of squares throughout. Place the paper under a board to relax it a bit while you pattern your colors. (Spanish Moire is generally done over a Stone or Rock pattern.)

Lay the paper as you would for a regular Spanish marbling pattern, coordinating your hand movements and moving even more slowly. If your paper is thin and you have a light in front of it, you may be able to see the squares contacting the color as the paper is laid. This can help you maintain confidence and concentration. Once mastered, this pattern will probably become one of your favorites—it's definitely a show-stopper at demonstrations!

"Pink And Green Moire" by Galen Berry, 25 x 19 inches (63.5 x 48.3 cm). Galen created this Spanish Moire design by folding a sheet of paper into squares and then laying it on the size with Spanish marbling techniques.

USING UNUSUAL MARBLING COMBS

Some marblers remove teeth here and there within a comb to create unusual patterned papers. Galen Berry's lovely balloon designs are the result of bending Nonpareil comb teeth out at odd angles and then using an up-and-down combing action.

To create the amazing work pictured below, Susan Pogány used a customized comb with some teeth spaced ½ inch (1.3 cm) apart and others spaced ¼ inch (0.6 cm) apart. She combed horizontally across color she'd previously applied in a series of horizontal bands. Next, using the handle of a teaspoon and starting at the bottom of the design, she pushed the colors upward in several spots to create what she describes as "mushroom-shaped creatures." Try distorting traditional designs by customizing your own tools and combing movements.

Detail of one of Galen Berry's signature "Balloon" designs

To create this amazing image, which she likens to little "mushroom-shaped creatures," Susan Pogány used a customized marbling comb and the broad handle of a teaspoon.

TROUBLESHOOTING

Dust spots

Excess ox gall or alum transferred to the size

Some of the more common problems encountered in watercolor marbling, and their probable causes, follow:

Color sinks when applied.

1. Your color may be too thick. Try thinning it with distilled water.
2. Your size may be too thick. If it clings to the marbled sheet and makes the sheet feel slimy after it's rinsed, the size should be thinned a bit with water of the same temperature. If this happens often, fill a jug with water and let it stand overnight in your marbling studio so it will be the same temperature as your size if you need it.
3. The color and size may not be the same temperature. If there are more than a few degrees difference between them, the color may sink.
4. Your color may not contain enough ox gall. If ox gall was, in fact, already added, you may not be stirring the color enough to distribute the ox gall into the color.
5. You may have applied your color too aggressively or in too large a droplet.
6. You may not have skimmed the size before applying the color. If a skin forms on the size, it can keep the color from spreading and floating.

Color expands and then contracts.

1. The temperature difference between the size and the color may be too great. If the size is cooler than the color, add a little warm water to the size.
2. The color may be too thick. Thin it by adding distilled water.

Colors shrink back from the edge of the tray. This often happens in dry weather or when the edge of the tray contains a buildup of skimmed color. To correct the problem, place a newspaper strip over the edge of the tray.

Color is grainy.

1. Some of the pigment may not be properly dissolved. Add a few drops of alcohol to help dissolve it.
2. The color may be sour or faulty. Label and save this batch for experimental work.
3. The color may be contaminated with dust, mold, or mildew. Save this color for wild experimentation.

Color runs during rinsing.

1. If all the color begins to rinse off, you've probably marbled the wrong side of the paper. Everyone does this at *least* once.
2. Your paper may be coated with calcium or may be so slick that it repelled the alum.
3. Your color may be too thick or was too aggressively applied.
4. Your alum solution may be too weak.
5. The size may be too old.
6. The size or color may be too cold.
7. The color and ox gall may not have been well mixed.

The marbled image appears fuzzy.

1. The size may be immature. Wait a few hours and try using it again.
2. The size, color, or both may be too thick. Dilute either (or both) with water of the same temperature.

The marbled image appears mushy and ill-defined.

1. The pattern may be overcombed. Try to have a clear idea of the pattern steps and movements you will execute before you begin manipulating colors.
2. The size may be too old or polluted to produce crisp patterns.

The marbled image has serrated or ragged edges.

1. Your size may be too thick or immature. See "The marbled image appears fuzzy," opposite.
2. A skin may have formed on the size, inhibiting proper color spread. Be sure to skim just before you apply your color.
3. The air may be too dry, contributing to a rapid skin buildup. Run a humidifier in your studio and try to work without air conditioning, which can dry the air.
4. Chemicals used to make your size or color may be affecting your colors. Try working with distilled water to see if it makes a difference.

Small specks and small globular voids appear in the marbled image.

1. Small white specks may be the result of dust or debris that wasn't skimmed off the size before you began applying colors (shown opposite, top).
2. Excess alum or ox gall may have transferred to the size (shown opposite, bottom). This can happen if papers are dragged over the edge of the tray when they're being picked up. Skim with a skim board a few times to remove pollutants, and then peel your papers back onto a rinse board to see if this corrects the problem.
3. Your alum may have crystallized on your paper. Check to see that your alum solution contains no crystals (if it does, reheat it to dissolve them) and that your aluming sponge contains no hardened crystals.
4. The tiny voids may be excess ox gall. Be sure to mix the ox gall thoroughly into your color.

Larger voids appear in the marbled image.

1. Large voids are caused by air bubbles. Make sure your papers are flat before marbling them. Getting more humidity into your workroom will make it easier to lay the papers.
2. Somewhat smaller voids are caused by air bubbles that form when paint hits the size. If these air bubbles plague you, check for them before you lay your paper down and pop them with a dry finger.

The marbled image contains blank streaks, blotches, or areas with faint patterns (shown at right).

1. You may not have alumed the paper properly. Next time, use overlapping strokes to make sure you don't miss any areas.
2. You may have marbled the paper while parts of it were still wet with alum.

Light or dark lines appear in the marbled image (shown at right).
You may have moved the paper during printing or allowed it to flop onto the size.

Colors rub off or chalk on dried papers.

1. There may be more color than can bind to the paper. Use less paint next time to avoid color buildup.
2. Slight chalking sometimes occurs with some manufacturers' paints. Try spraying the dried papers with an acrylic fixative of the type commonly used for sealing pastel drawings.

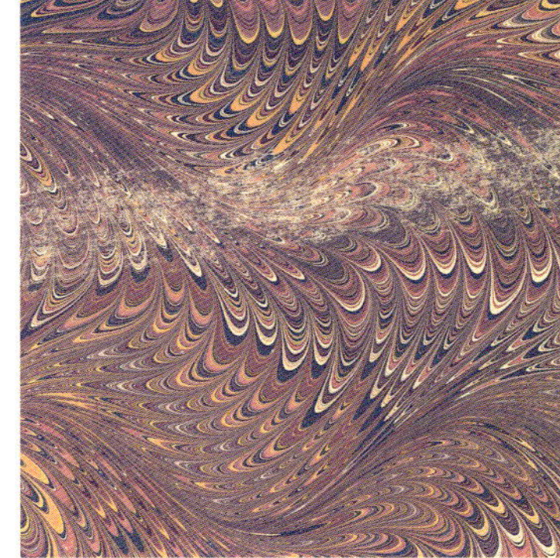

Unmarbled streaks caused by improper aluming

A dark line caused by unintentional paper-shifting

4 MARBLING FABRIC AND OTHER MATERIALS

MARBLING FABRIC

Fabric marbling, increasingly popular today, has been practiced for at least 200 years. Originally used to decorate book cloth for hand bookbinding, the technique is now used for all sorts of clothing, from sneakers to silk scarves. Marbled fabric is also in great demand for quilts, fabric tapestries, and decorative screens.

Most of the techniques described in the chapters on suminagashi, oil color marbling, and watercolor marbling also apply to fabric marbling. In fact, it's a good idea to familiarize yourself with marbling on paper before attempting designs on fabric. Handling and laying flexible lengths of fabric can be a bit more difficult than working with paper.

CHOOSING A FABRIC TO MARBLE

Many different types of fabric can be marbled. Silk, synthetic satin, cotton, cotton broadcloth, linen, and cotton knits all marble well. The synthetic fabrics seem more cooperative than some of the more loosely woven natural fabrics, which yield a fuzzier image. When choosing a fabric, be sure that it does not contain treatments such as fire retardants, dirt repellents, or permanent-press finishes, as they will cause problems. Try using some colored fabrics to expand your palette of colors. Be aware, however, that the hue of the fabric (especially darker fabrics) will show through the paint to create a third color.

Cantankerous paint actually enhanced this double-image acrylic-marbled design by the author

TESTING AND PREPARING FABRICS

To prepare your fabric for marbling, wash and thoroughly rinse it to remove any sizing that may be present. Silk may also contain sericin, a natural gum formed in the silk-making process. A product called Synthrapol, available at fabric supply houses, can be used to wash out any sericin prior to marbling. You'll also need to iron the fabric to remove any wrinkles, and to check the fabric for stray threads that can interrupt a marbled pattern.

Some fabric houses sell prewashed, unadulterated fabric for marbling or hand painting, but these may be more expensive. Before buying yards of any fabric, try marbling various swatches with each of the different marbling techniques to see how you like the results.

An acrylic-marbled floral scarf by Iris Nevins

CREATING A FABRIC MARBLING TRAY

You'll undoubtedly want to build a new, larger tray for fabric marbling. If you intend to marble scarves, you'll probably want a long, narrow tray. First determine the size of the scarves you intend to marble and then add a few inches leeway all around. Give yourself enough to room maneuver in, but not so much that excess color accumulates around the fabric and has to be skimmed off. You might also consider creating a tray wide enough to marble two or three scarves at a time.

To create a large makeshift tray with little effort, nail some two-by-fours together to form a frame. Then tack or staple the edges of plastic sheeting (at least 3.5 mm thick) to the top of the frame. (The plastic should be attached loosely enough to form a bowl for the size and floating colors.) At the 1989 Marbling convention in Santa Fe, we used this technique to create the world's largest makeshift marbling tray. Combed designs are not recommended for use with this type of tray, as comb teeth may puncture the plastic. (To build a longer-lasting tray, modify the instructions on page 16.)

HANDLING FABRIC

You'll have little difficulty marbling fabric if you have an assistant. This person can take one end of the fabric to be marbled and carefully lay it on the floating colors as you do the same. You and your partner must, however, work in unison. If you inadvertently lay your end down first, or pull the fabric toward you as you're laying it down, the indiscretion is sure to show in the finished piece. This may not be a disaster if you're working with several yards of fabric, but if you're marbling a hemmed silk scarf, it can be an expensive mistake. It's good to practice on plain water first, to get all movements synchronized.

If you intend to work solo, you'll need a set of thin dowels or bamboo rods with a pin at each end (the ready-made ones are called *shenshi*). These dowels or rods can be inserted into the rolled hem or selvage of the fabric. Some marblers also use pins or clothespins to attach the fabric to the dowels or to strips of balsa wood. To apply the fabric, grasp the dowel or rod at each end of the fabric. Let the center of the cloth droop down to touch the floating color, then smoothly lower the ends onto the color. This can be tricky, especially if you're trying to lay the fabric on a combed design. It's hard to keep your hands steady when your arms are outstretched. You may want to reserve these solo techniques for working with oil or

This great oil-marbled work was a joint effort produced by attendees from around the world at the 1989 Marbling Convention in Santa Fe, New Mexico. It was created in the world's largest makeshift marbling tray. (Photo by Diane Brady)

suminagashi images, in which mistakes are not so immediately recognizable, and ask for help when executing the combed acrylic designs.

Embroidery hoops are handy to use for isolating parts of fabric to be decorated with a marbled circle or oval. When you marble the circle of fabric within the hoop, hold the rest of the cloth up out of the way so it doesn't contact the color. These circular designs can be especially effective on T-shirts.

Sheets of waterproofed cardboard or rigid plastic are also helpful supports for marbling T-shirts. If you cut them to fit and slip them inside the shirt before marbling, they'll make the shirt more rigid and easier to handle. It's a good idea to make the cardboard form a little larger than the shirt, so that the shirt is stretched out when the support is inserted. This will assure that the marbling color covers the fabric thoroughly when the shirt is worn. The cardboard will also keep the marbling paint from bleeding through the shirt to the other side.

If you're working in a large tray, you may be able to just flip the shirt over onto the rest of the floating color to marble the other side. If your tray isn't this large, marble one side of the shirt and then reapply your color. Marble the other side in a similar pattern, being careful to slowly tip it onto the floating color to avoid trapping air bubbles.

SUMINAGASHI MARBLING ON FABRIC

Boku Undo inks, previously mentioned as useful for suminagashi marbling on paper (see page 17), also work exceptionally well on fabrics. To use Boku Undo inks on fabric, first prepare the fabric as discussed in the section "Testing and Preparing Fabrics" (see page 119). Because you're working on water, it will be helpful to have someone assist you if you're marbling a scarf or other length of fabric to keep it from shifting as you lay it down. For particularly gorgeous silks, try creating double- or even triple-image prints with suminagashi techniques. Because the Boku Undo colors are absorbed into the fabric, rather than simply placed on its surface, no curing time is necessary. Just rinse well and iron the marbled fabric. You can marble a prehemmed silk scarf or handkerchief in the morning and wear it by afternoon.

Suminagashi-marbled silk

OIL COLOR MARBLING ON FABRIC

To oil marble fabric, make a carrageenan or methyl cellulose size as described for oil color marbling on paper (see page 36), or float your oil colors on plain water for a more fluid look. Mix and apply your paints as suggested for oil color marbling, using whisks, eyedroppers, dropper bottles, or brushes (see page 38).

If you are working on a size, comb the colors. Otherwise, let the colors expand and form their own designs. Apply your fabric, choosing one of the techniques previously mentioned, and let the fabric rest on the size for a moment to make sure it has been saturated with all the floating color.

Rinse the fabric by gently swishing it in a large tub of cool or lukewarm water. Then carefully squeeze out the water and hang the fabric to dry. If you are marbling a T-shirt, leave the cardboard in place and gently hose off the fabric. When you're sure no color will migrate to the reverse side of the shirt, remove the support. Oil colors should cure for a couple of weeks, during which time most of the paint and paint solvent fumes will dissipate. After the colors have set, hand-wash and iron the fabric between two pieces of cotton broadcloth.

Some of the materials and equipment used for fabric marbling

An oil-marbled scarf and earrings by Sandra Holzman

Detail of an oil-marbled silk quilt with beading by Kay Radcliffe (work in progress)

An acrylic-marbled charmeuse jacket, skirt, and blouse in Bouquet and Rock patterns by Laura Crandall

FABRIC MARBLING WITH ACRYLICS

Because most watercolor paints and inks cannot be washed, they should not be used on fabrics that are meant to be worn. Some brands of fabric paints can be used, but most fabric marbling is done with acrylic paints. Although technically a water-based medium, acrylic paints are waterproof when dry. They come in an array of brilliant colors and can be floated on either a carrageenan or methyl cellulose size. (Acrylic paints can also be used for marbling on paper. Because acrylics are water-based, most of the techniques discussed for watercolor marbling on paper [see Chapter 3] can also be applied to acrylics.)

An unfortunate side effect of the quick-drying property of acrylics is that they tend to quickly form a rubbery consistency on marbling tools. This means that any residue of paints in marbling combs or color applicators will be difficult to remove. In addition, using tools with an acrylic residue for traditional watercolor marbling will cause spots and voids to appear in a pattern. For this reason, many acrylic marblers apply their paints with dropper bottles to minimize cleanup problems and build or buy equipment that they reserve for acrylic marbling only.

Many brands of acrylic paint can be used for marbling both paper and fabric. Paints made by Deka, Liquitex, Colorcraft, Pro Chem, and Decorative Papers, in both tube and liquid form, are all fine to use. If you're just starting out, you can minimize problems by purchasing paints especially prepared for marbling from a marbling supplier.

PREPARING ACRYLIC COLORS

To prepare acrylics not already formulated for marbling, you'll need to thin your paint with distilled water to about the consistency of thin cream. Then, in a separate testing tray, check the colors to see if they will float on the prepared size. Many acrylics will float and spread without difficulty. (In fact, the rogue colors that can't be tamed for marbling usually spread way too much, causing other colors to sink.) If most of the colors work well together, but a few tend to sink or get squeezed in by other colors, add a little diluted Photo-Flo to the problem colors to

Laura Crandall using a small dropper bottle to apply acrylic colors to a carrageenan size

help them float. Sometimes applying the colors in a different sequence will also help them stay afloat. To inhibit the spread of colors that expand too much, try adding a little distilled water to the colors or applying a small amount of a color that tends to spread too little.

If a color appears gritty or mottled it may mean that the pigment has separated from its binder. The solution is to remix the color and binder until they're well homogenized. One marbler friend attaches a whisk to a power drill and uses it to remix colors with fine results. Another way to smooth out gritty color is to add some acrylic medium to your paint, up to about 25 percent of the volume of the color.

ALUMING THE FABRIC

Before fabric (or paper) can be marbled with acrylic paints, it must be treated with an alum solution to make it receptive to the colors. For most fabrics, a solution of about 10 tablespoons (150 ml) of alum to 1 gallon (3.8 l) of water will help the fabric retain color well. Mix the solution as noted for watercolor marbling (see page 63). Pour the alum solution into a clean bucket or container, increasing the volume if necessary to accommodate several pieces of fabric. The fabrics should have room to relax and float and not be tightly bunched together. The alum must be able to reach all parts of the fabric so that the fabric takes color evenly when marbled.

Although some thicker fabrics may need to soak in an alum bath for up to half an hour, most lightweight fabrics, like silk and cotton, can be put in the bath, stirred slightly with a large spoon or dowel to be sure all parts of the fabric have been wetted, and removed after five minutes or so. Wear heavy vinyl gloves when removing the fabric to prevent the alum from irritating your hands.

Hang the fabric to dry by clipping it to an indoor clothesline. Place newspaper below the line to catch the alum solution as it drips from the fabric. It's important to make sure that the fabrics are not touching each other or wrapped around themselves as they dry. If the fabric does not dry in a single layer, the color will take unevenly and streaks will appear. (Outdoor drying is not recommended because the wind will usually cause fabric to roll back and stick to itself.) When the fabrics are dry, iron them to remove any wrinkles before marbling.

(Note: You should marble and rinse alumed fabrics within a day or two of aluming them. Alum left in fabric for any length of time will cause the fabric to decompose.)

APPLYING THE COLORS

Skim the surface of the size and then apply your colors. Although some fabric marblers apply their colors with brushes or eyedroppers, most use small 2-fluid ounce (59-ml) dropper bottles with good results. When using bottles, I try to make a habit of recapping them as soon as possible to prevent the acrylic paint from drying over the opening of the bottle. I always keep a straight pin handy to unplug any clogged bottles.

Because acrylics tend to be quite heavily pigmented, you may experience some color sinkage. A smaller dropper bottle and a gentler approach to color application may help lessen the problem. Remember that the correct way to use a dropper bottle is to keep pressure on the bottle so as not to draw air into it as you work. Also, it's important to hold the bottle close to the surface of the size when you release the drop of color. The few droplets of color that may sink to the bottom of the tray are unlikely to cause problems unless you stir them up with the teeth of your comb or rake as you pattern the colors. If you wish, you can easily remove these droplets by sucking them up with an eyedropper.

PATTERNING THE COLORS

Acrylics can be applied in Stone patterns (see page 72) or patterned with some of designs discussed for watercolor marbling (see pages 73–99). If you've never worked with acrylics before, start with some simple patterns in three or four colors that can be made rather quickly. If the acrylic color sits on the surface of the size too long, it may begin to dry, causing the pattern to break up. On the plus side, dust is not as much of a problem as with traditional watercolor marbling and, if you apply acrylic techniques to paper marbling, you'll find that colors will not chalk or offset when dry.

The author patterning acrylic colors with a stylus

Laura Crandall creating a Nonpareil design over a Gel Git pattern. (Laura prefers to create her Nonpareil and Bouquet pattern, which follows, by pushing her comb away from her rather than by pulling it toward her.)

Laura creating her Bouquet pattern with acrylic paints on a carrageenan size

APPLYING THE FABRIC

Apply your fabric as previously mentioned (see "Handling Fabric," pages 120–121) and let it rest on the surface of the color until the fabric becomes saturated, ensuring that the pattern has transferred to the fabric. (On silk, this takes only a second or two.) Then carefully pick up the fabric, trying to keep paint from running over onto the reverse side, and place it in a large bucket of cold water. At this point the marbled image is still a very fragile surface design that can be marred by touching it. I usually lift the fabric with my hands on its unmarbled side, and then transfer it to another large bucket of water. Let the fabric float freely for a few minutes to rinse out excess alum and size before hanging it on a line to dry.

When the fabric is completely dry and the design is a little less fragile, rinse the fabric again, swishing it around a bit. Let the fabric dry a second time, and then iron its unmarbled side to set the color. Depending upon what type of paint you use, the manufacturer may suggest ironing or heat-setting the color in a dryer. Most acrylic-marbled fabrics will still not be totally cured for at least another week or so. After this time, fabrics that feel stiff can be softened by soaking them in water with fabric softener.

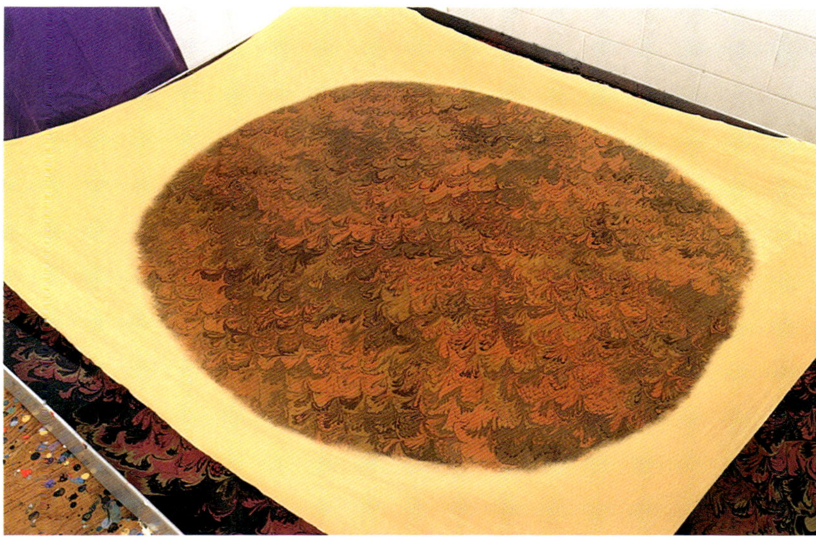

Laura and a helper laying fabric on a completed Bouquet pattern

The marbled fabric being removed from the size. It is now on its way to the rinse bucket.

SKIMMING

Before another piece of fabric can be marbled, you must carefully skim the size to remove all residue of acrylic paint. Adequate skimming is essential to successful acrylic marbling. The acrylics that remain after a print is made sometimes sink just below the surface of the size and sit there, waiting to impede the spread of new colors applied. For this reason, it's important to get in the habit of routinely skimming several times with a skim board or, better yet, skimming simultaneously with a skim board and newspaper skim strip. Any time colors that previously floated begin to sink, set the skim board at least ¼ inch (0.6 cm) below the surface of the size to skim. Many problems you may encounter with acrylics sinking, beading, or breaking up can be easily corrected by deeply skimming a few times.

CARING FOR MARBLED FABRICS

Most marbled fabrics can be hand-washed in a mild soap solution or dry-cleaned without losing their color. It's safest to soak the fabrics, rather than scrub them, to remove any soil since they bear surface designs that can be disturbed by rough handling. For the same reason, fabrics should be gently squeezed to remove water rather than wrung out.

ALTERING THE IMAGE WITH ADVANCED TECHNIQUES

Many of the advanced techniques noted in previous chapters can be adapted for use on fabric. Although lightweight fabric can't be folded to create shifted designs, you might try ironing canvas into folds and oil marbling it. Marie Palowoda has had some success creating shifted designs on silk by attaching the fabric to a paper backing that facilitates laying it down (see below, left). Fantasy design techniques can also be applied, as in the silk scarf shown on page 119, which Iris Nevins decorated with a series of marbled floral images.

EXPLOITING THE NATURE OF ACRYLICS

Because acrylics tend to dry when exposed to air, deliberately letting them sit on the surface of the size for a few minutes before printing

Marie Palowoda's shifted design was accomplished by attaching silk to a paper backing, thereby making it more rigid and easier to handle.

"Marble Squared" by Sandra Holzman. This large 48- x 30-inch (121.9- x 76.2-cm) oil-marbled painting was created on a rayon-cotton blend satin. Sandra used common masking tape for the resist work and further embellished the piece with acrylic stamping.

them can yield some interesting patterns. The colors will often bead up or become grainy, looking more like oil colors. This can be annoying at some times, and welcomed as a useful design element at others.

OVERMARBLING

Overmarbling techniques are very effective on fabrics, such as on the scarves shown at right. If you're marbling fabric to be used as clothing, however, you'll want to consider the fact that each layer of oil paint or acrylic paint applied will tend to stiffen the fabric. Fabric softener will help somewhat, but repeated marbling can destroy the hand of some fine fabrics.

USING FRISKETS

Both frisket film and liquid frisket can be successfully used to create designs on marbled fabric. Be sure to test the frisket on a piece of fabric first to make sure it won't leave a residue when removed. Some marblers use heavy-duty waxed freezer-wrapping paper to create friskets for fabrics. Just cut out an image and iron it, wax-side down, on the fabric to be marbled. The photos of Sandra Holzman's and Kay Radcliffe's oil-marbled fabrics (shown on page 128 and below, respectively) show how frisket and overmarbling techniques can be combined with oil marbling to produce stunning designs.

Overmarbled scarves by the author. After being ironed to set the acrylic color, the scarves will hang for at least a week before being treated with fabric softener.

In this demonstration design by Kay Radcliffe, white frisket film has been applied to magenta fabric.

After marbling the fabric with gold paint, Kay removed the friskets. The areas not covered with film are rendered gold, while the areas covered with the film remain unmarbled.

TROUBLESHOOTING

For problems with suminagashi or oil colors spreading too much, too little, or sinking when applied, check the troubleshooting guides in those chapters (see page 28 for suminagashi inks and page 55 for oil colors). For problems specifically related to marbling fabric or marbling with acrylic paints, see below.

Colors form jagged shapes on the size.

1. You may not have skimmed the size properly and a skin or excess color may be interfering with color spread. Use the skim board to deep-skim the size. Getting more humidity in the marbling studio can also help keep a skin from forming.
2. Your size may be too thick. (Sometimes it will thicken as you work with acrylics.) Add some water to thin the size, making sure that the water is about the same temperature as the size.

Bubbles form on the size.

1. Are you using a dropper bottle or eyedropper to deposit color? Be sure to keep pressure on the bottle or bulb to avoid drawing in air, which then gets deposited on the size as a bubble. Try to pop the bubbles with a dry finger or, if there aren't too many, lift them off with a piece of newspaper.

A particular color runs when the marbled fabric is hung to dry.

1. The color may be too thick. This problem, particularly noticeable with metallic colors, can be corrected by thinning the offending color with distilled water or adding a bit of diluted Photo-Flo to help it spread more.
2. The color may have been squeezed into a tight line of concentrated color when another expanding color was applied over it. Adjust your colors, or the sequence in which they're applied, to help them cooperate more with each other.

Tiny solid beads and specks of color appear on the marbled fabric.

1. Oil color or acrylic color may have dried on the surface of the size. Skim well and try to work more quickly next time.
2. The paint may not have been properly mixed. Remix the paint to help it disperse properly.
3. Bits of dried pigment may be present in your paint. Strain the paint through a nylon stocking or coffee filter to remove the dried pigment, or add a little alcohol to help dissolve the pigment. Be sure to cover and recap paints when they're not in use.
4. If you've marbled several pieces of fabric, you may have deposited excess paint in your rinse bucket that is transferring to fabrics as you rinse them. Make sure your rinse water is clean. Check fabrics as they are hung to dry and pick off any bits of dried paint with the point of a twisted paper towel.

MARBLING OTHER MATERIALS AND OBJECTS

Almost anything that can fit in your marbling tray can be marbled. Giddy students in one of my classes proved that one day when they departed from paper marbling and began a contest to see who could marble the strangest object. Sneakers went on the size first, followed by checkbook covers and dollar bills. An older woman marbled her cane and then another student marbled a banana. One well-endowed student began laughing and leaned over her tray a bit too far, emerging with the prize-winning entry!

Although it's easiest to marble materials like wood, clay, slate, mirror, and leather with oil colors or acrylics, regular gouache-based watercolor paints can also be used, provided the material is first alumed. Alum water can be sprayed on objects or applied with a sponge.

Milena Hughes shown acrylic marbling the center panel for a residential foyer floor. Notice how Milena has used newspaper to block off part of her tray and control color spread.

MARBLING SHEETS OF WOOD

Fine-grained hardwoods will marble well. Softer woods can be marbled if they are first coated with a sealer and then roughened up a bit with fine steel wool. (If you are planning to marble with watercolors, you would then need to alum the wood before marbling.)

To marble a flat piece of wood, position it parallel to the size. Let one edge make contact with the marbling color and slowly lower the rest of the wood onto the size. This is a bit tricky—if you apply the wood at too slight an angle, you run the risk of trapping an air bubble and ruining your design. Many flat wooden pieces are overmarbled for this very reason.

To manage large pieces of wood, you'll have to devise a set of handles like those created by Milena Hughes, shown working on a six-tile center panel for a wooden foyer floor she was commissioned to produce.

MARBLING BOWLS AND OTHER CURVED OBJECTS

Wooden bowls and other curved objects can be rolled onto a marbled pattern or lowered into a container so that the pattern wraps itself around the object. Work slowly so you don't create a wake that pushes the color aside.

Milena Hughes, whose "Lacewood Bowl with Embroidery Marbling" is pictured on the next page, has created some beautiful acrylic-marbled bowls. To produce the bowl shown, she created rings of color on a carrageenan size and compressed the colors with a skim board, moving them to one-half of her marbling tray. When the colors expanded again, Milena rolled the bowl through the lacy bands of color. Milena let the color overlap into the bowl for a less controlled look. She notes: "The wood was so beautiful that I only wanted an interesting band of color to compliment the wood pattern and not cover it entirely. Also, the shape of the

"Lacewood Bowl with Embroidery Marbling," by Milena Hughes, now in the collection of marbling historian Phoebe J. Easton. The 3½- x 5¼-inch (8.9 x 13.3-cm) bowl was made by Geof Hiltwein.

Hikmet Barutcugil used mineral dyes and oil pigments to marble this vase. Mineral dyes are plentiful in Turkey, a country rich in natural metal oxides, where the dyes are made by filtering and crushing earth.

bowl reminded me of a Japanese rice bowl, so I chose a design that would emphasize and enhance an oriental theme."

It's always wise to choose your marbling colors carefully to avoid destroying a beautifully turned wood piece. A gentleman came to my classroom at a large crafts school one day, asking me to marble a cherry bowl he'd made in a neighboring woodworking class. I couldn't imagine destroying the subtle color changes in the wood with opaque paints, but finally agreed to marble it with diluted Boku Undo suminagashi colors. He wanted me to use red, yellow, blue, green, and purple on the piece. We finally compromised and I, holding my breath, slowly lowered the bowl into a bucket of water on which I'd floated rings of pale red, yellow, and orange dyes. We both wound up pleased. The subtle marbling enhanced the work, accenting the natural beauty of the wood.

Bisque-fired or clay pottery, slate, and stone will also accept marbled images. If you're using watercolors or acrylics, remember to alum the object first. An acrylic sealer may be used to protect the surface of objects marbled with traditional gouache-based paints.

When using oil paints, no pre- or postmarbling treatment is necessary. The gorgeous vase shown at left, marbled by Hikmet Barutcugil, was simply plunged into a deep tank containing floating mineral dyes and oil pigments.

MARBLING GLASS AND MIRROR

Very smooth or highly polished surfaces have to be slightly roughened before they will accept an alum mordant (necessary for marbling with any materials other than oil paints). Prepare such surfaces by applying several coats of a mat fixative or by scouring them with steel wool. After marbling, you may want to protect your images by coating them with an acrylic spray.

MARBLING BOOK EDGES

Many antique books not only have marbled endpapers and/or cover papers, but marbled fore edges as well. The custom of marbling fore edges arose for several reasons. For example, frequently consulted books, such as dictionaries and encyclopedias, didn't show hand oils as much if their fore edges were marbled. Even more important, ledgers and record books could be easily monitored for tampering if the edges of the books were marbled, as page removal would immediately form a break in the marbled pattern. Marbled fore edges probably discouraged many would-be thieves.

Marbling was usually done before the book was cased (given a cover). Often, the top and bottom edges of the book were marbled along with the fore edge. If you want to try marbling the fore edge of a book, lift the book covers out of the way and clamp the book's pages together with boards held by C-clamps. Lightly scour the clamped edge with steel wool to remove dirt and oils. If using watercolor paints, blot an alum-soaked sponge against the fore edge to be marbled.

Apply the clamped edge to the marbled pattern, rinsing it by spraying it with water, if necessary. Keep the book clamped until dry and then fan the pages to separate them.

Paul Maurer used frisket film to preserve an unmarbled center for this watercolor-marbled mirror. After marbling, the patterned area was coated with an acrylic sealer.

Watercolor-marbled endpapers and edges shown on A Life of Lord Lyndhurst, *published in 1883. The marbled pattern is called Spotted Antique with Curl. (From the collection of Phoebe Jane Easton.)*

5

A GALLERY OF CONTEMPORARY MARBLING

THE ART OF MARBLING continues to evolve as more and more artists adopt marbling as their primary medium. Increasing numbers of artists are also using marbling in conjunction with other fine art disciplines, like collage, drawing, and painting. The following selection of work by various artists presents innovative explorations of color, composition, and texture.

"Reef" by the author, 27 x 23 inches (68.6 x 58.4 cm). Multiple-image gouache marbling on a carrageenan size.

"Untitled," from the New Growth Series by Milena Hughes, 18 x 22 inches (45.7 x 55.9 cm). Acrylic marbling on a carrageenan size.

"The Crucible" by Tom Leech, 18 x 24 inches (45.7 x 61 cm). Acrylic marbling with friskets and foil on handmade paper.

"Agate Chun-Ki" by Milena Hughes, 1½ x 4 inches (3.8 x 10.2 cm). Acrylic marbling on a carrageenan size. Maple bowl lathe-turned by Geof Hiltwein.

"Paris" by Christopher Weimann, 19 x 24¾ inches (48.3 x 62.9 cm). Acrylic and gouache marbling on a guar gum size.

"Once Upon a Time" by the author, 11 x 14 inches (27.9 x 35.6 cm). Collage of paste papers, orizomegami papers, handmade papers, and watercolor-marbled papers.

"Rainforest Sunset" by Jennifer Philippoff, 20 x 24 inches (50.8 x 61 cm). Collage of cut paper, suminagashi-marbled papers, and oil- and ink-marbled papers made on a carrageenan size.

"Beech Tree and Rocks" by Dedree Drees, 32 x 16 inches (81.3 x 40.6 cm). Watercolor and watercolor-marbled collage.

"Echoes" by Susan Pogány, 18 x 12 inches (45.7 x 30.5 cm). Watercolor marbling on a carrageenan size.

"Turkish Flower over Barut Ebru" by Hikmet Barutcugil, 19⁷⁄₁₀ x 13⁴⁄₅ inches (50 x 35 cm). Mineral dyes and pigment color marbling on a gum tragacanth size.

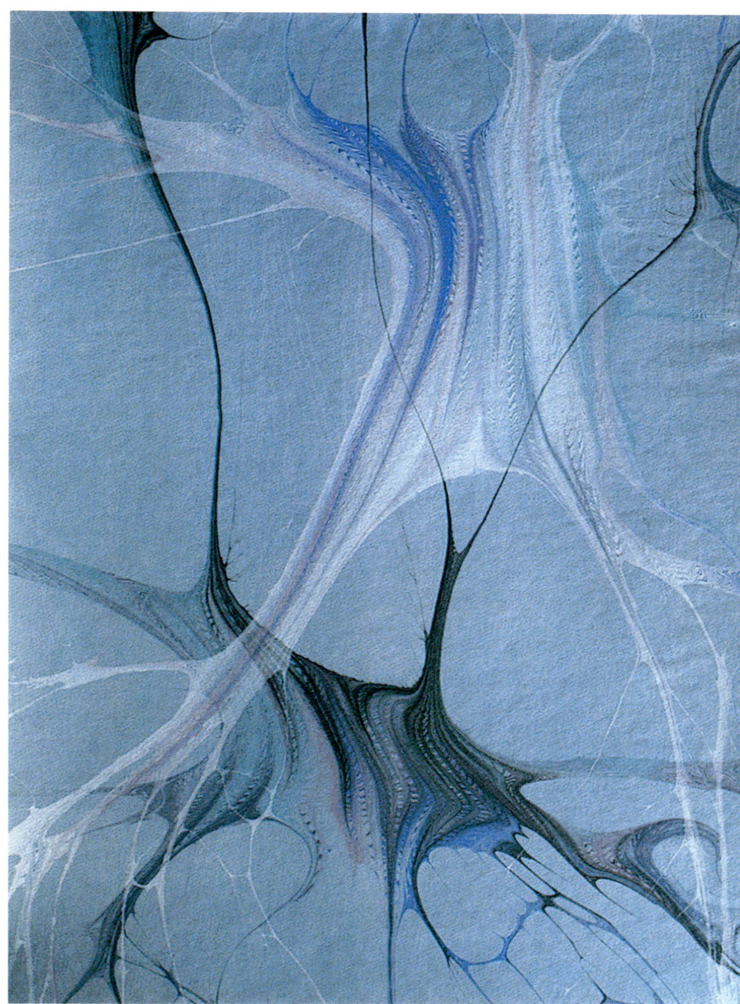

"Forces" by Susan Pogány, 24 x 18 inches (61 x 45.7 cm). Overmarbled watercolor on a carrageenan size.

"Snow Seasons" by Paul Maurer, 18 x 24 inches (45.7 x 61 cm). Painting with collage of oil marbling on a carrageenan size.

"Untitled" by Eva van Breugel, 22 x 28⅓ inches (55.8 x 71.9 cm). Watercolor marbling on a carrageenan size.

Paper sculpture for a children's book illustration by Hal Lose, 18 x 24 x 2 inches (45.7 x 61 x 5.1 cm). Watercolor-marbled papers on a carrageenan size.

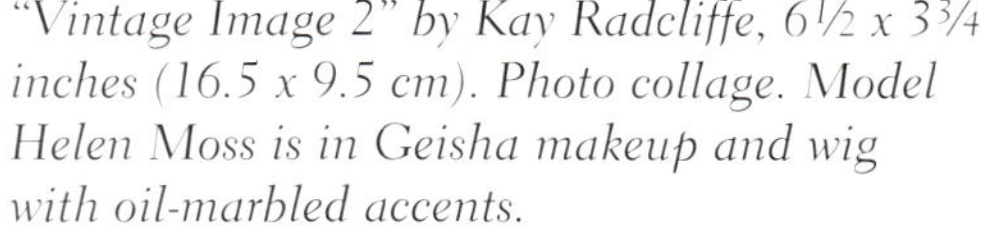

"Vintage Image 2" by Kay Radcliffe, 6½ x 3¾ inches (16.5 x 9.5 cm). Photo collage. Model Helen Moss is in Geisha makeup and wig with oil-marbled accents.

"Buck" by Galen Berry, 25 x 19 inches (63.5 x 48.3 cm). Overmarbling with frisket work. Acrylic marbling on a carrageenan size.

"Paint Can Lid" by Christopher Weimann. Leather dyes on the lid of a metal paint can.

"Shades of Spain" by Mimi Schleicher, 18 x 18 inches (45.7 x 45.7 cm). Watercolor marbling on a carrageenan size.

Further Reading

Some of the books listed below are out of print, but you may be able to find copies in larger libraries. Copies of out-of-print books may also be available directly from the author.

Chambers, Anne. *Suminagashi: The Japanese Art of Marbling: A Practical Guide.* New York: Thames and Hudson Inc., 1991.

Easton, Phoebe J. *Marbling: A History and a Bibliography.* Los Angeles, CA: Dawson's Book Shop, 1983.

Grünebaum, Gabriele. *Techniques for Marbleizing Paper.* New York: Dover Publications, Inc., 1992.

Guyot, Don. *Suminagashi: An Introduction to Japanese Marbling.* Seattle: Brass Galley Press, 1988.

Halfer, Josef. *The Progress of the Marbling Art.* Buffalo: American Bookbinding Co., 1894. (Reprinted: Taos, NM: Fresh Ink Press, 1989.)

Loring, Rosamond B. *Decorated Book Papers.* 3rd ed., Cambridge, MA: Harvard College Library, 1973.

Maurer, Diane and Paul. *An Introduction to Carrageenan and Watercolor Marbling.* Spring Mills, PA: Diane Maurer, 1984.

Maurer, Diane, with Paul Maurer. *Marbling: A Complete Guide to Creating Beautiful Patterned Papers and Fabrics.* New York: Crescent Books, 1991.

Maurer-Mathison, Diane, with Jennifer Philippoff. *Paper Art.* New York: Watson-Guptill Publications, 1997.

Miura, Einen. *The Art of Marbled Paper: Marbled Patterns and How to Make Them.* London: Kodansha International Ltd. and Kodansha America, Inc., 1991.

Nevins, Iris. *Traditional Marbling.* Sussex, NJ: Iris Nevins, 1985.

Nevins, Iris. *Varieties of Spanish Marbling.* Johnsonburg, NJ: Iris Nevins, 1991.

Weimann, Ingrid and Nedim Sönmez. *Christopher Weimann (1946-1988): A Tribute.* Tübingen, Germany: Jäckle-Sönmez, 1991.

Weiss, Franz. *The Art of Marbling.* (Translated from the German with samples by Richard J. Wolfe). North Hills, PA: Bird & Bull Press, 1980.

Source Directory

Listed at right are the suppliers for many of the materials used in this book.

Marbling Supplies

Colophon Book Arts Supply
3611 Ryan Street, Southeast
Lacey, WA 98503
(360) 459-2940
E-mail: colophon@olywa.net

Diane Maurer Hand Marbled Papers
P.O. Box 78
Spring Mills, PA 16875
(814) 422-8651
E-mail: dkmaurer1@aol.com
Source for traditional marbling supplies and Boku Undo colors

Iris Nevins Decorative Papers
P.O. Box 429
Johnsonburg, NJ 07846
(908) 813-8617
E-mail: irisnevins@compuserve.com

TALAS
568 Broadway
New York, NY 10012
(212) 219-0770
E-mail: talas@sprynet.com

Paper

Daniel Smith, Inc.
4150 First Avenue South
Seattle, WA 98134
(800) 426-6740
E-mail: dsartmtrl@aolcom

Dick Blick
P.O. Box 1267
Galesburg, IL 61402
(800) 447-8192
http://www.dickblick.com

New York Central Art Supply, Inc.
62 Third Avenue
New York, NY 10003
(800) 950-6111
http://www.nycentralart.com

Pearl Paint Co., Inc.
308 Canal Street
New York, NY 10013
(800) 451-PEARL
http://www.pearlpaint.com

Stephen Kinsella, Inc.
P.O. Box 32420
Olivette, MO 63132
(800) 445-8865

Local art supply shops and printers in your area are also a good source for papers.

Fabrics and Scarves

Qualin International
P.O. Box 31145
San Francisco, CA 94131
(415) 333-8500

Rupert, Gibbon & Spider, Inc.
P.O. Box 425
Healdsburg, CA 95448
(800) 442-0455
E-mail: jacquard@sonic.net

Test Fabrics, Inc.
415 Delaware Ave.
P.O. Box 26
West Pittston, PA 18643
(717) 603-0432
E-mail: testfabric@aol.com

Thai Silks
252 State Street
Los Altos, CA 94022
(800) 722-SILK
http://www.thaisilks.com

INDEX